Country Inn Meals to Remember

by GAIL GRECO

Based on the PBS-TV Series *Country Inn Cooking with Gail Greco*

ILLUSTRATED BY *Trish Crowe*

RUTLEDGE HILL PRESS

NASHVILLE, TENNESSEE

Companion to the public television series *Country Inn Cooking with Gail Greco,* a co-production of Maryland Public Television and Gail Greco.

Published in Nashville, Tennessee, by Rutledge Hill Press, Inc., 211 Seventh Avenue North, Nashville, Tennessee 37219. Distributed in Canada by H. B. Fenn & Company, Ltd., 34 Nixon Road, Bolton, Ontario L7E 1W2. Distributed in Australia by The Five Mile Press Pty. Ltd., 22 Summit Road, Noble Park, Victoria 3174. Distributed in New Zealand by Tandem Press, 2 Rugby Road, Birkenhead, Auckland 10. Distributed in the United Kingdom by Verulam Publishing, Ltd., 152a Park Street Lane, Park Street, St. Albans, Hertfordshire AL2 2AU.

Illustrated by Trish Crowe

Book design by Harriette Bateman

Typesetting by D&T/Bailey Typesetting, Inc., Nashville, TN 37203

Front and back cover photography by Tom Bagley
All recipes selected and edited for the home kitchen by Gail Greco

Recipes featured on the front cover: Applewood-Smoked and Rosemary Cornish Hens, Baked Trout Bundles with Watercress Sauce, Raspberry Coulis Cloud

Cover Photo: Gail Greco at The Inn at Vaucluse Spring, Stephens City, VA

Library of Congress Cataloging-in-Publication Data

Greco, Gail
    Country inn meals to remember : based on the PBS-TV series More country inn
    cooking with Gail Greco / Gail Greco ; illustrated by Trish Crowe.
       p.   cm.
    Includes index.
    ISBN 1-55853-538-1 (pbk.)
       1. Cookery, American   2. Bed and breakfast accommodations—United States.
    I. More country inn cooking with Gail Greco (Television program)   II. Title.
    IN PROCESS
    641.5973—dc21   97-31747
                                                                                        CIP

Printed in the United States of America

1 2 3 4 5 6 7 8 9 — 99 98 97

Contents

. . . That Great Country Inn Spirit
Introduction   vii

Acknowledgments   v

Mornings to Celebrate *1*

FABULOUS BREAKFASTS AND SPECIAL BRUNCHES

All In An Afternoon *47*

SALADS, SANDWICHES, TEA-TIME SWEETS

A Light at the Inn *67*

APPETIZERS, ENTRÉES, SIDE DISHES, DESSERTS

Always of Service *131*

PANTRY STAPLES

Inn Directory   147

Resource Directory   158

Inndex   177

Other Books by Gail Greco

Country Inn Cooking

The Romance of Country Inns

Tea-Time at the Inn

Great Cooking with Country Inn Chefs

Secrets of Entertaining from America's Best Innkeepers

Breakfasts and Brunches

The World Class Cuisine of Italy and France

GAIL GRECO'S LITTLE BED-AND-BREAKFAST COOKBOOK SERIES:

Autumn at the Farmers Market

Chocolates on the Pillow

Gardens of Plenty

Recipes for Romance

Tea-Time Journeys

Vive la French Toast!

To my dear friends Nancy and Peter Fanelli, for some of my most cherished meals ever, and for always being there and staying so close to my heart in spite of the distance . . . Mom and Dad are forever grateful.

... *That Great Country Inn Spirit*

I thought by now—after countless published articles about bed-and-breakfast and country inns and their food, many books on the subject, a television show, and many personal appearances cooking inn food and telling others how many wonderful things inns can do for you—that I would be a bit weary of this topic. But as I perused those articles with my bylines dating back to the early eighties, re-read my books, watched some of the shows, remembered some of the cooking demonstrations I gave (and still give) all over the country on behalf of inn recipes, I realized that I have not become jaded but am still enthralled by the spirit of country inn lodgings and the travel and adventure that goes along with them.

I continue to hold the belief that innkeepers are today's true experts in hospitality and entertaining and they have become even more important and creative—even trendsetting in their mass numbers—at helping us all to bring lifestyle virtues home with us, particularly when it comes to what goes on in the kitchen. Recipes for fabulous breakfasts, warm afternoon teas, and enchanted evenings are probably brought back from inns more than from anywhere else. Decorating and gardening tips and even ideas on how to live the romantic life come along with the fine cooking. The inn environment is a breeding ground for fertile ideas to live life to the fullest every day, and that includes learning to enjoy and make more time for cooking and turning every meal at home into a special event.

The bed-and-breakfast topic is not the only reason why I am spurred on to bring the essence of country inns home for all of us. You have written to me and told me that you watch the show faithfully and that your books have become dog-eared from use. I know that I have succeeded by your feedback and encouraging words to go on. That is my motivation to continue in this same vein.

To that end, in 1997 I established the first-ever culinary association of small inns. *The Cooking and Baking Association of Bed & Breakfast and Country Inns* (along with the Professional Association of Innkeepers International) is intended to continue to raise the consciousness level of the traveler and general public as to the virtues and talents of those cooking at the bed-and-breakfast and country inns. The message goes out that inns provide fresh, homemade food in intimate atmospheres—an ambience with which other lodging styles cannot compete. The association believes that the serving of food to the traveler—whether it be breakfast, lunch, afternoon tea, dinner, or any other—is an essential part of the bed-and-breakfast/country inn experience.

As I put this book together to accompany the third broadcast season of *Country Inn Cooking with Gail Greco,* I did so with the same enthusiasm I had with my very first book many years ago. In keeping with tradition, I have included recipes from inns all across the country, with an emphasis on regional cooking. We keyed on the cuisine of the plantation South; the rugged and hearty menus of the mountainous West; the carefree but traditional meals of the Pacific Northwest; the varying regional tastes of New England; the old frontiers of Alaska and Hawaii; and paid special attention to Mid-Atlantic hamlets, tucked away for the discriminating traveler and food lover.

Images come to mind of visits during the show such as in the Wild West town of Julian, California, where folks line up "amid the cotton-weed" for slices of homemade apple pie sold in more than three busy bakeries in two small village blocks; and how innkeeper Kay Minns's filling breakfast was what we needed to go mushing in Wyoming dogsled country. I recall the splendor of a night as king and queen watching the moon eclipse the turret as we enjoyed a medieval meal at Ravenwood Castle in the Ohio countryside and how we visited my own hometown of Annapolis, Maryland, for a lesson in crabbing on the Chesapeake in this city that was the capital of the United States a few centuries ago.

Viewers told me that some of their favorite episodes were those where we did more breakfast fare. So in this new series we produced a show devoted only to breakfast, called *Morning Glories.* And in the main series, nine of the twenty-six shows feature breakfast fare. All of the recipes that I and the country inn chefs cooked for you on television are here for you to create with ease and love in your own kitchen. So, with this book and the new episodes of the show, I think I can say that for myself and all of the featured chefs and inns on the series, we are there with you in that great country inn spirit as you enjoy these delicious recipes.

Country Inn Meals to Remember
by GAIL GRECO

Cheese & Vegetable Filled Egg Blossom Crepes

MORNINGS TO CELEBRATE

Fabulous Breakfasts and Special Brunches

Fruit

Port Wine Fruit Compote

If you have ever been to Portugal, you can understand how special a recipe is when it incorporates port wine in the list of ingredients. Portugal, the home of port winemaking, is a lovely and romantic part of the world. Making this at the Inn at Maplewood Farm is even more special as Jaymes Simoes, the innkeeper, hails from Portugal and still has family there. Your own guests will truly enjoy this superb version of a traditional morning fruit dish. This recipe is served as a first breakfast course, or it may be served with dessert, such as with ice cream.

1 pound mixed dried fruits (figs, cranberries, apples, prunes), chopped into bite-sized pieces
Grated rind of 1 lemon
Grated rind of 1 orange
1 cinnamon stick

1 large dried bay leaf
2 cups tawny port wine (ruby port is a bit too sweet for this dish)
1 cup water
½ cup or less fresh orange juice

Stir together all of the above ingredients except for the orange juice in a nonreactive saucepan. Heat and simmer the mixture uncovered for 1 hour, stirring occasionally. Add the orange juice to the mixture slowly and as needed to keep the fruit soft but the mixture not too liquid. When the fruit is soft and the compote is of a thick consistency, remove from the heat, cover, and let cool to room temperature. Remove and discard the cinnamon stick and the bay leaf. Serve either warm or cool.

    Makes 6 servings

    — *THE INN AT MAPLEWOOD FARM*

Spiced Peach Soup

Refreshing and simple to make, this eye-opening soup can also be served in a tall glass. Add a decorative glass stirrer.

1¼ cups water
⅓ cup B&B liqueur, optional
⅓ cup sugar
6 large fresh peaches, washed, pitted, peeled, and sliced

1 teaspoon ground cinnamon
½ teaspoon ground ginger
¼ teaspoon grated nutmeg
¾ cup fresh orange juice
Edible violets for garnish

In a large saucepan, blend the water, liqueur, and sugar to make a simple syrup. Bring to a boil. Add the peaches, cinnamon, ginger, and nutmeg. Cover and simmer for 20 minutes. Remove the mixture from the heat; add the orange juice and place in a blender. Blend until smooth. Pour into small bowls. Float violets in the center of the soup and serve chilled. (Soup may also be heated and served warm.)

Makes 6 servings

— *THE INN AT MAPLEWOOD FARM*

Strawberry-Cantaloupe Side-by-Side Soup

When strawberries are in season and the cantaloupe is sweet, this soup, served side by side in a bowl, brightens the morning table and makes for an impressive breakfast appetizer that is very low in calories.

CANTALOUPE SOUP
1 medium-sized cantaloupe, peeled, seeded, and coarsely chopped
1 cup fresh orange juice
½ cup quality nonfat vanilla yogurt

STRAWBERRY SOUP
2 cups chopped, hulled fresh strawberries
1 cup fresh orange juice
½ cup quality nonfat vanilla yogurt
   Edible flowers for garnish

In a blender, purée all of the ingredients for the cantaloupe soup until smooth; set aside. Repeat for the strawberry soup. Pour each soup alternately into chilled bowls, cantaloupe on one side and the strawberry on the other. (You may also swirl the two together, just at the top surface.) Garnish each serving with an edible flower.

Makes 8 servings

— *THE INN AT MAPLEWOOD FARM*

Creamy Watermelon-Raspberry Soup

Start the recipe the night before serving. The watermelon is frozen so that it keeps the soup well chilled (almost like having ice cubes in the glass).

4 cups chopped seedless watermelon
1 cup fresh or frozen raspberries
1 tablespoon honey

1 cup heavy cream
   Grated rind of 1 lime
   Fresh mint leaves for garnish

Place the chopped watermelon in the freezer and freeze overnight. In the morning, place the watermelon, raspberries, and honey into a blender. Purée, and scrape the sides of the blender as necessary. When the fruit is smooth, add the cream and process again until smooth. Divide the soup among 6 small, chilled soup bowls. Sprinkle each serving with grated lime rind. Garnish each with a mint leaf.

Makes 6 servings

— *THE INN AT MAPLEWOOD FARM*

Anise-Scented Blueberry-and-Peach Compote

The slight hint of anise laces the fruit combination, offering a tasty, clean and refreshing fragrance.

6 cups water	2 tablespoons aniseeds
6 medium fresh peaches	1½ cups fresh blueberries
2 cups water	Dollop of sour cream for
⅔ cup sugar	garnish

Bring the water to a boil. Drop the peaches in the boiling water and boil for 1 minute. Remove the peaches and peel off the skins. Slice each peach into ¼-inch thick-slices, removing the pits. In a medium-sized nonreactive saucepan, boil the 2 cups water, the sugar, and the aniseeds together until the sugar dissolves. Stir frequently. Boil into a syrup until the mixture reduces to 1 cup, about 15 to 20 minutes. Remove the mixture from the heat and strain off the aniseeds. Pour the warm syrup over the peaches and toss. Add the blueberries, stirring gently. Refrigerate the compote overnight and serve cool at breakfast with a dollop of sour cream, if desired.

Makes 6 servings

— THE INN AT MAPLEWOOD FARM

Breads, Pies, Cereals

Early-American Savory Breakfast Toasts

Early American receipt (recipe) books often had a chapter devoted to making toast entrées, meaning topping bread with an assortment of sweet or savory combinations and then toasting them open-face under a broiler. Perhaps the best known of these is Welsh rarebit (or Welsh rabbit) where cheddar cheese is combined with dry mustard and beer and melted and poured over toasted white bread. Here is an assortment of recipes that inn owner and cook Robert Zuchelli adapted from Marion Cunningham's The Breakfast Book. William Page Inn, being an historic home, is the perfect setting for such a mirror image of morning meals gone by. These are easy to prepare and make a nice dish for everyday at home, even for lunchtime.
    Makes 2 servings

Sausage Applesauce Toast

¼ cup cooked quality breakfast sausage
2 slices toasted and buttered rye bread

½ cup (sweetened or unsweetened) applesauce

Crumble sausage over each piece of bread. Cover with the applesauce and place under the broiler for about 1 minute (watch carefully). Serve immediately.
   — WILLIAM PAGE INN

Apple-and-Cheese Toast

2 tablespoons butter for
  sautéing
1 apple, any style, peeled, cored,
  and thinly sliced

2 pieces any type bread, toasted
  and lightly buttered
⅓ cup grated cheddar cheese

Melt the butter in a small skillet and add the apple slices. Cook over
low heat for 3 to 4 minutes, or until the apple is tender. Pour the
mixture evenly over the bread. Sprinkle the cheese over the apple
and place under the broiler just until the cheese has melted. Serve
immediately.
— *WILLIAM PAGE INN*

Tomato-and-Herb Toast

3 tablespoons butter
6 tablespoons fresh bread
  crumbs
1 teaspoon chopped fresh basil,
  sage, or any desired herb

1 cup chopped fresh tomatoes
  Salt and pepper
2 slices crusty Italian bread,
  toasted and buttered and
  sprinkled with garlic powder

In a small skillet, melt half of the butter and lightly brown the bread
crumbs, stirring constantly. Remove the bread crumbs from the pan
and mix in the herbs. Add the remaining butter to the skillet and stir
in the tomatoes. Add salt and pepper to taste. Spread the tomato-herb
mixture over the bread and top with the bread crumbs. Place under
the broiler for 30 seconds or so and serve.
— *WILLIAM PAGE INN*

Sweet Potato Biscuits with Orange Butter

Sweet potatoes are a staple food of the South, and there's nothing more southern than homemade biscuits. This recipe calls for mashed sweet potatoes. The non-yeast batter needs to rest for 4 hours.

BUTTER
½ cup (1 stick) butter
2 teaspoons honey
2 teaspoons grated orange rind
1 edible flower

BISCUITS
3 cups mashed sweet potatoes (approximately 2 large potatoes baked and mashed)
½ cup sugar
¾ cup (1½ sticks) butter, softened
4 cups all-purpose flour
1 teaspoon salt
3 teaspoons baking powder

In a small bowl, combine all of the butter ingredients (except the flour) well. Press into a 3½-inch ramekin or other small container. Garnish with the fresh flower and refrigerate.

In a large bowl, mix together the potatoes, sugar, and the butter. In a separate bowl, combine the flour, salt, and baking powder. Add the mixture to the potatoes and stir to combine. Cover and let stand at room temperature for at least 4 hours. Preheat the oven to 400°. Roll out to 1-inch thick on a floured surface. (If dough is too sticky, work in more flour.) Cut with a 2-inch biscuit cutter and place biscuits on a lightly greased baking sheet 2 inches apart. Bake for 15 to 20 minutes, or until a tester comes clean. Serve hot with the orange butter.

Makes 2 dozen

— THE ASHLEY INN

Glacier Bay-gels

Wednesday is bagel day at the Glacier Bay Country Inn. Baking starts at eight o'clock in the morning so that the bagels are still fresh and warm in time for lunch. Everyone gets involved in the baking process, and the innkeepers enjoy the help, as well as the company. "By lunchtime, you're lucky if there are any bagels left—the inn is crawling with bagel thieves!" laughs Chef Jon Emanuel. Some of the staff's favorite bagel varieties follow this basic recipe.

DOUGH	SIMMERING SOLUTION
4 cups bread flour	1½ gallons water
1 tablespoon active dry yeast	¼ cup sugar
1½ cups warm water	2 teaspoons kosher salt
2 tablespoons sugar	
1½ teaspoons salt	

Start by making the dough. Into the bowl of an electric mixer, spoon 2 cups of the flour and the yeast. Add the warm water, sugar, and salt. Mix with the dough hook attachment until the ingredients come together. Add the remaining 2 cups of flour and continue kneading. If the dough is too sticky, add a bit more flour. Knead for 10 minutes. Dough should be firm and not too sticky. Remove the dough from the mixture and place on a floured surface. Cover loosely with a kitchen towel and allow the dough to rest for 10 minutes, or until 1½ times its original size.

Meanwhile, prepare the simmering solution. Combine all of the solution ingredients in a deep roasting pan and bring to a high simmer.

Preheat the oven to 425°. Divide the dough into 12 equal portions. With floured hands, roll the dough pieces into balls. Using your fingers, poke a hole through each and stretch the dough out evenly, about 3 inches. Place the rings directly into the simmering solution. Simmer for about 2 to 3 minutes, or until the bagels float. Remove the bagels from the solution and place directly onto a greased baking sheet. Allow them to rest for about 5 minutes, then bake in the oven for 5 minutes. Decrease the oven temperature to 375°. Continue baking for 10 more minutes.

Makes 12 Ba-gels

VARIATIONS:

SESAME SEED, POPPY SEED BAGELS:

Just prior to baking, brush the bagels with beaten egg and sprinkle on seeds or your favorite topping.

SUN-DRIED TOMATO-AND-BASIL BAGELS:

Add ½ cup rehydrated chopped sun-dried tomatoes and 2 tablespoons chopped basil to the dough just before you are finished kneading. Continue kneading until all ingredients are combined.

GINGER-AND-GREEN ONION BAGELS:

Add 3 tablespoons freshly grated ginger and ⅓ cup chopped green onions to the dough just before you are finished kneading. Continue kneading until all ingredients are combined.

JALAPEÑO-AND-CHEESE BAGELS:

Add ½ cup chopped jalapeños and ½ cup grated cheddar cheese to the dough just before you are finished kneading. Continue kneading until all ingredients are combined.

—*GLACIER BAY COUNTRY INN*

Breakfast Cookies

Here is just the morning meal to take with you as you run out the door with coffee in your thermal mug.

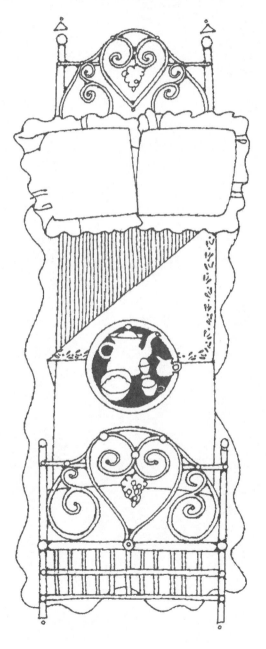

1¼ cups all-purpose flour	½ cup soft-style margarine
⅔ cup sugar	1 egg
½ cup granola	2 tablespoons frozen orange
½ pound quality country-style bacon, cooked, drained, and crumbled	juice concentrate, undiluted
	1 tablespoon grated orange rind

Preheat the oven to 350°. In a large mixing bowl, slowly mix together the ingredients in the order they are listed. Stir until well blended. Drop by the level tablespoon 2 inches apart on lightly greased cookie sheets. Bake for 10 to 12 minutes, or until golden. Remove from the oven immediately to a wire rack to cool.

Makes 2½ dozen

— *THE SOUTHERN HOTEL*

Sausage, Apple, and Cheese-Curried Cornbread Pudding with Pumpkin Sauce

Innkeeper Sally Krueger literally came up with a winner when she developed this recipe for a Jones Dairy Farm competition, featuring the company's quality sausage. The pudding is divine. I know; I was one of the judges! The uniqueness of this dish almost brought tears to my eyes. Look at the list of ingredients and see how expertly the items complement one another like a symphony, each playing off the other in perfect harmony. The pudding makes a great entrée, or consider half the suggested serving for a side dish. You will need to make the cornbread a day ahead of time. See page 135 for a cornbread recipe.

1 small onion, finely chopped	SAUCE
12 ounces bulk sausage	2 cups puréed pumpkin
Ground black pepper, divided	2 cups skim milk
4 cups day-old cornbread cubes	¼ cup packed brown sugar
3 cups shredded mozzarella cheese	Fresh mint for garnish
10 eggs	
2½ cups skim milk	
1 teaspoon ground coriander	
½ teaspoon ground cumin	
¼ teaspoon ground ginger	
⅛ teaspoon dry mustard	
¼ teaspoon curry powder	
4 Granny Smith apples, cored and thinly sliced	

Preheat the oven to 350°. In a large skillet, sauté the onion and sausage over medium-high heat until cooked through, about 3 minutes. Stir in about ¼ teaspoon pepper; remove the pan from the heat. Drain the sausage well and pat dry with a paper towel. Set aside.

Coat 2 muffin tins (total of 24 cups) with nonstick cooking oil spray. Divide the cornbread cubes evenly among the muffin cups. Next, evenly layer the sausage-and-onion mixture, followed by the cheese. Set aside.

In a medium mixing bowl, mix together the eggs, skim milk, coriander, cumin, ginger, mustard, curry powder, and about ⅛ teaspoon of ground black pepper until well incorporated. Pour ¼ cup of the egg-milk mixture into each muffin cup. Top each cup with 3 apple slices arranged in a layered pattern around the top of the batter. Bake uncovered for 25 minutes, or until the pudding is set. Remove from the oven and let the pudding sit for 5 minutes before serving. Meanwhile, prepare the sauce.

Place the pumpkin sauce ingredients into a small saucepan. Stir the ingredients and cook over medium heat until heated through.

Run a knife around the edge of the muffin cups. For each serving, carefully remove 2 puddings and set out on a plate. Place a pool of pumpkin sauce on the side of the plate. Garnish with a sprig of mint.

Makes 24 puddings (12 servings)

— *THE INN AT 410*

Papaya Bread Pudding

Fresh papaya grows not too far from Gloria and Bob Merkle's enchanting inn on the ocean. Almost any toasted bread will do for the base of the pudding; toast by placing cubes into a 350° oven for about 6 to 8 minutes. Papaya seeds are also great toasted and added to a salad or cereal. Substitute mango if papaya is unavailable.

PUDDING
- 3 to 4 cups toasted bread cubes
- 2 cups milk
- 6 eggs, beaten
- 1½ cups sugar
- ¼ teaspoon salt
- 1½ teaspoons ground cinnamon
- ½ cup raisins, optional
- 1 cup seeded and puréed papaya
- ½ cup diced papaya
- 2 teaspoons vanilla extract
- ½ cup pecans or almonds

SAUCE
- 1 cup seeded and diced papaya
- 1 cup half-and-half
- ½ cup honey
- 4 teaspoons fresh lemon juice

GARNISHES
- 12 broiled pineapple rings
- Whipped cream
- Mint leaves

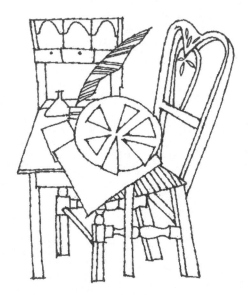

Begin by making the pudding. Preheat the oven to 350°. Mix all of the pudding ingredients and pour into a baking dish 9 x 13 inches. Place a larger pan of water under the baking dish for a water bath. Bake the pudding on the bottom shelf of the oven for 40 to 45 minutes, until pudding is set and a tester comes clean.

Meanwhile, prepare the sauce. Combine all of the sauce ingredients in a blender and process until smooth. Heat just to warm. Cut individual portions of the pudding and top with the sauce. Garnish each serving with 2 broiled pineapple rings, whipped cream, and a sprig of mint.

Makes 6 servings

— *GLORIA'S SPOUTING HORN B&B INN*

Breakfast Calzone

Innkeeper Kate Nieman makes a habit of coming up with creative break-fast entrées. She has won recipe competitions for her efforts, including a first-place and third-place award from Jones Dairy Farm. I think this recipe is bound for headlines as well. You may want to serve this with the Italian Eggplant Salsa on page 142, also made by Kate.

2 (12 ounces each) packages all-natural bulk sausage
4 cups ricotta cheese
2 eggs
Salt and pepper
⅛ teaspoon freshly grated nutmeg
½ cup finely chopped Italian parsley
½ cup freshly grated Parmesan cheese
¾ cup chopped sun-dried tomatoes
4 packages crescent rolls (4 sheets crescent roll dough)
12 hard-boiled eggs, thinly sliced
Egg wash for topping

Preheat the oven to 375°. In a large skillet, brown the sausage, breaking it up into small pieces. Drain and cool completely.

Drain the ricotta cheese into a large bowl. Add the 2 eggs, salt, pepper, nutmeg, parsley, and Parmesan cheese, stirring until thoroughly combined. Fold in the cooked sausage and the sun-dried tomatoes. Set aside.

Arrange 2 crescent-roll sheets across the width of a jelly-roll pan, pulling the dough up along the sides. Using your hands, pat down the dough to fit, making sure that the perforated seams are closed. Spread the sausage-and-cheese mixture evenly over the crust. Place the boiled egg slices in a layer over the sausage-and-cheese mixture. Top with the remaining 2 crescent roll sheets, patting down to fit the pan and closing the seams. Moving around the pan, pinch the edges of the dough together to seal. Brush the calzone with the egg wash (*see* page 28) and prick the top crust several times with a fork.

Cover with aluminum foil and bake for 20 minutes. Remove foil and bake for another 10 minutes or until golden brown. Allow the calzone to cool for at least 15 minutes before slicing into squares. Serve warm with a fresh-fruit compote.

Makes 10 servings

—*WASHINGTON HOUSE INN*

Good Morning Pizza

Pizza first thing in the day may seem a little out of place except when it is this version from innkeeper Barbara Hankins's kitchen. The pizza allows you to enjoy entertaining your guests while it bakes in the oven.

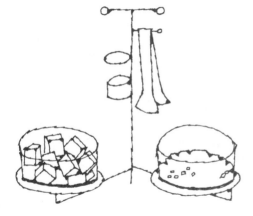

PIZZA

- 3 ounces crumbled breakfast sausage
- ½ cup small-diced green bell pepper
- 1½ cups packaged shredded hash-brown potatoes
- 4 eggs, beaten with 2 tablespoons water
- 2 green onions, chopped, including tops
- 1 ready-made pizza shell or refrigerated pizza dough, cooked
- 1 medium fresh tomato, seeded and cut into ½-inch dice
- Salt and pepper
- ½ cup shredded Swiss cheese

SAUCE

- 1¼ cups skim milk
- 2½ teaspoons cornstarch
- ½ teaspoon chicken bouillon granules
- 1 teaspoon Dijon-style mustard

Stir together the milk, cornstarch, and chicken bouillon over medium heat until thickened and bubbly. Blend in the mustard and set aside.

Sauté the sausage and green pepper in a small skillet until browned; drain and set aside. Prepare the hash browns according to package directions. Preheat the oven to 375°.

Cook the eggs and sliced green onions in a nonstick medium skillet. (Do not stir until the eggs begin to set.) Lift and fold the eggs, so that the uncooked portion runs under the set portion. Continue cooking for 1 or 2 minutes until the eggs are set but still glossy. Remove from the heat.

To assemble the pizza, spray a pizza pan with nonstick cooking oil spray. Arrange the dough in the pan. Cover the dough to within an inch or less of the edge with the hash browns. Follow with the eggs on top, then the sausage and peppers, tomato, and salt and pepper to taste. Top with the sauce and then the cheese. Bake for 12 to 15 minutes, or until heated through.

Makes 6 servings

— *THE SOUTHERN HOTEL*

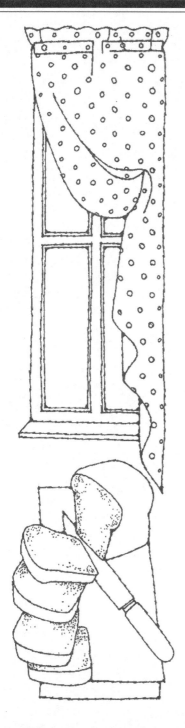

Pancake Pizza with Macadamia Nut Crust and Banana-Sour Cream Topping

When I first stepped foot onto Gloria's B&B, it was late at night and I had been flying for 13 hours to get to Kauai from the East Coast. I could not see outside my room, but I knew I was in a very special place. Outside my window, the moonlight hinted at palm trees, and I could hear their gentle swaying eclipsing the surf. Next day, I was outside my window, lolling in a hammock. If I were you, I would book my flight to Gloria's as soon as possible, or at least put this recipe together and go there vicariously.

TOPPING
6 to 8 small bananas
- ¾ cup brown sugar
- 1 tablespoon butter, melted
- 1 cup sour cream

PANCAKE
- 2 eggs
- 1¾ cups milk
- 2 tablespoons salad oil
- 1 teaspoon maple flavoring
- 2 cups pancake mix of choice
- ¾ cup granola (preferably without raisins)
- ¾ cup macadamia nuts (pecans, walnuts, or almonds may be substituted)

Preheat the oven to 375°. Peel the bananas and cut into ½-inch slices. Place the fruit in a shallow glass baking dish 9 x 13 inches. Sprinkle brown sugar evenly over the top of the bananas. Pour the melted butter over the brown sugar and bananas. Bake in the oven for 30 minutes, or until browned. Remove the fruit from the oven and spread the sour cream over the top. Keep the bananas warm in the oven while preparing the pancakes.

Increase the oven temperature to 425°. In a large bowl, beat the eggs, milk, and oil. Add the maple flavoring and blend. Add the pancake mix and beat the mixture by hand until smooth. Coat the inside of a 14-inch pizza or paella pan or baking pan 10 x 15 inches with nonstick cooking oil spray. Pour the batter into the pizza pan. Sprinkle the granola and the macadamia nuts evenly over the batter. Bake the pizza on the bottom rack of the oven for about 12 to 15 minutes, or until a tester comes clean. Cut the pie into wedges and serve with the banana-sour cream topping.

Makes 6 servings

— *GLORIA'S SPOUTING HORN B&B INN*

Morning Cheese Pie with Creamed Crabmeat

Special egg and French toast dishes are the usual order of the day at William Page Inn, but here inn owner and cook Robert Zuchelli adds a bit of regional flavor with fresh crabmeat in a sauce that is baked around cheese-and-pimento-stuffed pinwheels.

CRABMEAT
- 3 tablespoons butter
- 2 small onions, finely chopped
- 1 medium-sized green bell pepper, seeded and cut into small dice
- 5 tablespoons all-purpose flour
- ½ teaspoon salt
- 2⅔ cups milk
- 2 cups lump crabmeat
- 1 tablespoon lemon juice

CHEESE ROLLS
- 1½ cups all-purpose flour
- 1 tablespoon baking powder
- ½ teaspoon salt
- 3 tablespoons shortening
- ½ cup milk
- ¾ cup shredded cheddar cheese
- ¼ cup chopped pimento

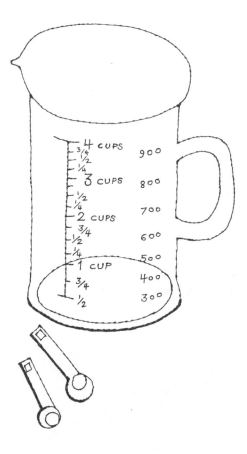

Grease a 2-quart baking dish. Set aside.

To make the creamed crabmeat, melt the butter in a medium-sized saucepan. Add the onion and green pepper. Cook for a few minutes, just until the vegetables are tender. Stir in the flour and the salt. Slowly add the milk, mixing well to incorporate. Remove from the heat and keep stirring until the mixture is thickened and bubbly. Stir in the crabmeat and the lemon juice. Pour the mixture into the prepared baking dish. Set aside and make the cheese rolls.

In a medium bowl, mix together the flour, baking powder, and the salt. Using a pastry blender, cut in the shortening. Add the milk and stir just until the dough clings together.

Preheat the oven to 425°. Turn the dough out onto a lightly floured surface. Knead gently for 10 to 12 strokes. Roll the dough out into a rectangle 12 x 8 inches. Sprinkle the cheese and then the pimento over the dough. Roll up lengthwise. Cut the roll into 8 equal slices. Slightly flatten each slice with your hand. Place the pinwheels, spiral sides on top, around the crabmeat-filled baking dish. Bake for about 25 minutes, or until golden brown. Let the pinwheels stand for 10 minutes before serving.

Makes 6 servings

— *WILLIAM PAGE INN*

Granola-Peach Breakfast Pie with Yogurt Sauce

Make your own granola for this pie or rely on such quality granola makers as Walnut Acres, *an organic-products catalog company we featured on the show (see Resource Directory, page 158). Chef Scott Brouse at the Inn at Olde New Berlin uses Walnut Acres' Maple Almond Granola for this recipe. A granola with a similar nutty flavor and maple taste, will also do the job.*

CRUST
2½ cups maple-and-almond gra-
     nola or similar combination
  4 tablespoons butter, melted
¼ cup brown sugar
  2 egg whites

FILLING
  8 to 9 fresh peaches, skinned,
     pitted, and thinly sliced
⅓ cup sugar
½ teaspoon ground cinnamon
  5 tablespoons cornstarch

SAUCE
  1 cup heavy cream
¼ cup sugar
  2 egg yolks
1½ teaspoons all-purpose flour
1½ teaspoons vanilla extract
⅛ teaspoon salt
½ cup frozen yogurt, flavor of
     choice

Preheat the oven to 350°. Pour granola into a medium stainless-steel mixing bowl. In a 1-quart saucepan, over low heat, whisk together the melted butter and brown sugar. Add this mixture to the granola, blending well with a rubber spatula. Blend the egg whites into the mixture with the spatula. (The mixture will be thick.) Place the mixture into an ungreased 10-inch baking dish, spreading the granola evenly around the dish and up the sides to form a crust.

In another medium-sized mixing bowl, combine the peaches, sugar, cinnamon, and cornstarch. Pour the filling evenly over the granola crust. Bake for 25 to 30 minutes, or until peach mixture is set and granola crust is lightly browned. Remove from the oven and let cool.

While the pie cools, prepare the sauce. In a 1-quart saucepan, whisk together the cream and sugar over medium heat. Bring the mixture to a boil; reduce heat to warm.

In a small mixing bowl, whisk together the egg yolks, flour, vanilla, and salt until smooth. Pour the entire mixture into the saucepan. Cook over very low heat. Stir constantly with a wooden spoon until the mixture begins to thicken, about 8 to 10 minutes (do not boil). Remove from the heat. Stir in the frozen yogurt until it is melted; serve at room temperature. Serve spooned over the pie.

Makes 6 to 8 servings

— *INN AT OLDE NEW BERLIN*

Baked Cranberry Oatmeal

Almost like a granola, but softer and creamier, this unusual baked oatmeal proves that you can do a lot with cereal to make a special dish. Substitute cherries, blueberries, or raisins for the dried cranberries.

3 cups skim milk, plus more for serving if desired

6 tablespoons packed brown sugar

1½ tablespoons margarine

2 teaspoons ground cinnamon

1½ cups old-fashioned oats

1½ cups peeled, finely chopped Granny Smith apples, plus ½ Granny Smith unpeeled and sliced for garnish

¾ cup dried cranberries

¾ cup coarsely chopped walnuts or pecans

Preheat the oven to 350°. Coat a 9-inch-square pan with nonstick cooking oil spray.

In a large saucepan, bring the milk, brown sugar, margarine, and cinnamon to a boil. Meanwhile, in a large mixing bowl, mix together the oats, chopped apple, cranberries, and nuts; spread evenly into the prepared pan.

When the milk mixture begins to boil, pour out evenly over the oatmeal mixture. Bake uncovered for 30 to 35 minutes, or until the liquid has been absorbed and the oatmeal is tender. Cut the mixture into 6 servings, scooping each out into a cereal bowl. Garnish with the sliced apple and serve with a pitcher of skim milk.

Makes 6 servings

— *THE INN AT 410*

Apricot-Almond Couscous

It is not that easy to find breakfast dishes for vegetarians as so many such recipes call for meat, eggs, and dairy products. But here is one dish, vegan or otherwise, that tastes so good and may be substituted in place of oatmeal. Creative innkeeper Sally Krueger showed this on the air, but many more of her wonderful recipes are in her cookbook Mountain Mornings, *available from the inn.*

2 tablespoons chopped slivered almonds
2 tablespoons unsweetened shredded coconut
4 dried apricots
1 teaspoon honey, optional

2 tablespoons plus ¾ cup boiling water
¾ cup couscous
Cinnamon for garnish
Fresh fruit for garnish

Preheat the oven to 350°. Spread the almonds and coconut onto a large flat baking sheet and toast in the oven until golden brown, about 10 minutes. Set aside to cool.

Chop the apricots into small dice and place in a small bowl with the honey and the 2 tablespoons of the boiling water. Let sit until the apricots are softened, about 10 minutes.

About 5 minutes before serving, pour the couscous into a medium bowl. Add the ¾ cup of boiling water and cover tightly with plastic wrap. Let sit for 5 minutes. After 5 minutes, uncover the couscous and fluff up. (If the couscous is still hard, cover again, and let steam for another minute or so.)

Drain the liquid from the apricots and discard. Stir the apricots into the couscous. Divide the couscous between 2 plates or bowls. Sprinkle with a little cinnamon and top each plate with half of the roasted nuts–coconut mixture. Serve warm, garnished with fresh fruit.

Makes 2 servings

— *THE INN AT 410*

Charleston Shrimp 'n' Grits

The inn admits that many people find shrimp with grits an unusual combination at first. But after they finish breakfast at the Ashley Inn, believers are born. Shrimp is a breakfast favorite in the Low Country, the coastal region stretching from Myrtle Beach to Beaufort. Grits, the ground grain of corn is a very popular side dish all over the South. When accompanied with the shrimp—well! Stone-ground grits are coarser than most and preferred in this recipe as they have a better flavor and consistency than regular grits.

GRITS
- 4 cups water
- 2 tablespoons butter
- 1 cup stone-ground grits
- 2 to 3 cups heavy cream or half-and-half

GRAVY
- 8 slices lean bacon
- 3 tablespoons finely chopped onion
- 2 tablespoons finely chopped red bell pepper
- 2 tablespoons finely chopped green bell pepper
- 2 cups raw small to medium-sized shrimp, peeled
- 2 teaspoons Worcestershire sauce
- 2 teaspoons ketchup
- 2 to 3 drops Tabasco sauce Salt and pepper to taste
- 1½ cups water
- 2 tablespoons all-purpose flour Chopped parsley for garnish

Begin by cooking the grits. In a heavy 2-quart saucepan, bring the water to a boil. Add the butter and then stir in the grits. Reduce the heat and allow the grits to simmer, stirring occasionally, until most of the water is absorbed, about 10 minutes. Add the cream, ½ cup at a time, as the grits continue to cook. The total cooking time will be about 1 hour. The grits should be just slightly soupy but full-bodied.

While the grits cook, fry the bacon until crisp. Remove the bacon from the pan and drain. Fry the onion and the peppers in the bacon grease until soft. Add the shrimp and cook until pink, just a few minutes. Add the Worcestershire sauce, ketchup, Tabasco, and salt and pepper to taste. Add 1 cup of the water. Mix the flour with the remaining ½ cup water until smooth and pour into the sauce to thicken. Chop the bacon and add half of it to the shrimp gravy. Serve over the grits and garnish with the remaining chopped bacon and parsley.

Makes 4 to 6 servings

— *THE ASHLEY INN*

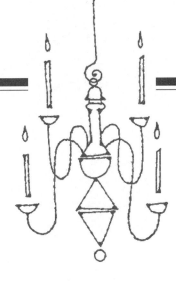

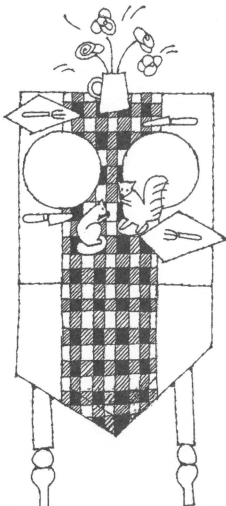

Eggs

Sun-Dried Tomato-and-Bacon Popover Pancake

These puffy baked pancakes look and taste like sweet oversized popovers. They make a lot of various popovers for breakfast at the inn, but here innkeeper Sally Krueger combined the flavors of smoky bacon and tangy dried tomatoes to create this unique, savory version of a "Dutch baby" with a unique yogurt sauce. Use a heavy cast-iron skillet or special steel oven–pancake pan for puffiest results.

SAUCE
⅓ cup plain nonfat yogurt
⅓ cup light sour cream
2 teaspoons chopped fresh basil
2 teaspoons chopped fresh Cilantro
1 teaspoon chopped fresh mint
1 tablespoon olive oil
1 tablespoon Dijon-style mustard

PANCAKES
3 ounces sun-dried tomatoes (about 20 to 25 tomatoes)
1 pound quality sliced bacon
6 eggs
1 cup skim milk
2 tablespoons olive oil
1 cup all-purpose flour
½ teaspoon salt
2 large Roma tomatoes, thinly sliced
½ cup ½-inch-diced green bell pepper
½ cup ½-inch-diced yellow bell pepper

Prepare the sauce: In a small bowl, combine the yogurt, sour cream, basil, cilantro, mint, olive oil, and mustard until well blended; cover and refrigerate until ready to serve.

Preheat the oven to 400°. Place a heavy 10-inch-round pan in the oven to heat. Place the sun-dried tomatoes in a medium bowl. Pour enough hot tap water over them to cover; let sit until soft, about 15 minutes. While the tomatoes are softening, cook and chop the bacon. Drain well.

In a medium bowl, whisk the eggs by hand until frothy; add milk and olive oil and whisk to combine. Sprinkle in flour and salt. Beat until well mixed. Mixture will be very runny.

Remove the hot pan from the oven and coat with nonstick cooking oil spray. Reserve 2 teaspoons chopped bacon for use as garnish.

Spread the rest of the chopped bacon in the bottom of the pan; top
with the prepared sun-dried tomatoes. Pour the batter into the pan,
filling it about ⅔ full. Bake for 15 minutes. Reduce the oven temperature to 325° and continue to bake for 35 to 40 minutes more, or until
puffed and golden.

Immediately loosen the pancake from the pan and slide it onto a
serving dish. Garnish the center with the sliced tomatoes and sprinkle
with the green and yellow peppers. Cut into 6 wedges and serve
immediately with a dollop of the sauce and a sprinkling of the
reserved bacon.

Makes 6 servings

— THE INN AT 410

Oven Eggs Florentine

*Easy to prepare, this recipe is a true crowd-pleaser and it is picturesque,
especially when garnished with fresh fruit and herbs. The William Page
Inn uses its common parlor as the breakfast room. Guests take breakfast
on trays on their laps, and it makes for a friendly, personal atmosphere.*

18 eggs
2 cups small-curd cottage
  cheese
½ cup biscuit mix (such as
  Bisquick)
1 cup shredded Monterey Jack
  cheese

1 cup shredded Colby cheese
2 ripe plum tomatoes
1 cup freshly chopped spinach
3 finely chopped green onions
¼ cup (½ stick) butter, melted

Preheat the oven to 350°. In the large bowl of an electric mixer, blend
the eggs, cottage cheese, biscuit mix, and Monterey and Colby
cheeses. Mix at medium speed for 5 to 6 minutes. Add the tomatoes,
the spinach, and the onions. Add the butter and mix by hand until
blended.

Pour the egg mixture into a dish 9 x 13 inches that has been
coated with nonstick cooking oil spray. Bake for 50 to 60 minutes, or
until set but still moist. Remove from the heat and cool for 10 minutes. Cut into twelve 3-inch squares. Serve on a plate with garnish of
your choice and some ham or Canadian-style bacon.

Makes 12 servings

— WILLIAM PAGE INN

Herbed Shiitake Eggs in Homemade Pita Bread

Innkeeper Laura Simoes loves making this bread, and it showed while she demonstrated the easy process on camera. Although it is easier just to pick up a sack of pita bread at the market, the homemade-fresh version is chewier and thicker.

BREAD
- 2 packages (2 tablespoons) dry active yeast
- ¼ teaspoon sugar
- 2 cups warm water
- ¼ cup olive oil
- 6 cups quality hard-wheat flour that is high in gluten
- Cornmeal flour for sprinkling on baking sheets

In a large bowl, mix together the yeast, sugar, and warm water. Add the olive oil. Add the flour 1 cup at a time, stirring after each addition to form a dough. Turn the dough out onto an unfloured board and knead until smooth and elastic. Place the dough in a clean bowl and cover with a tea towel. Let rise in a warm place for 30 minutes. Punch dough down and divide it into 8 sections. Roll each section into a ball. Place dough balls on a wax-paper-lined baking sheet(s). Cover balls with a tea towel and let rest for 30 minutes. After 30 minutes, take each dough ball and flatten it out to 1/8-inch thick with a floured rolling pin, until it is about the size of an 8-inch circle. Dust 4 baking sheets with cornmeal and place 2 dough rounds on each baking sheet. Cover again with a tea towel and let rest for 30 minutes. Preheat the oven to 500° with a rack on the top shelf and a rack on the bottom shelf. After 30 minutes, the oven should be hot enough and the dough ready to be baked. Poke each dough round several times with a fork. Put a baking sheet on the top rack for 5 minutes, then move the pan to a lower rack for another 2 minutes. Spin the pan around and bake another 2½ minutes, or until pitas are puffed and lightly browned. The breads will deflate while cooling. Repeat with remaining baking sheets.

HERBED SHIITAKE EGGS

8 eggs

½ cup half-and-half

⅛ teaspoon white pepper

8 shiitake mushrooms, cleaned and thinly sliced

2 tablespoons snipped fresh herbs (chives and thyme are nice)

In a medium bowl, scramble the eggs with the half-and-half and the white pepper. Cook over medium heat in a nonstick skillet that has been lightly coated with nonstick vegetable oil spray. Stir occasionally. Add the mushrooms when the bottom of the pan is hot and the eggs start to cook. Sprinkle with the herbs. Continue to stir only occasionally. Remove the pan from the heat when the eggs are just set and let sit for a minute while you prepare the pitas for stuffing. Stuff 6 to 8 fresh pita halves with the egg mixture. Garnish each plate with a sprig of fresh herbs and serve.

Makes 8 servings

— *THE INN AT MAPLEWOOD FARM*

Egg-and-Potato Vegetable Tarts with Feta Cheese

The Victorians were famous for their duchess potatoes—puréed potatoes made with egg yolks and butter, and then usually piped as garnish or served as a side dish. Innkeeper Todd Seidl does just that in this recipe, which befits his Victorian-inspired B&B. The recipe calls for making individual egg tarts topped with basil, zucchini, bell peppers, and breakfast sausage.

POTATOES
  2 pounds white potatoes, peeled
    and quartered
  ¼ cup (½ stick) butter
    Salt and pepper
    Nutmeg
  3 egg yolks
    Egg wash (1 egg with 1 table-
    spoon cold water)

TOPPING
  2 tablespoons butter
  1 medium zucchini, sliced
    julienne
  ½ medium red bell pepper, sliced
    julienne
  ½ medium yellow bell pepper,
    sliced julienne

TARTS
  10 eggs, lightly beaten
  ⅓ cup cold water
  ¼ cup (½ stick) butter
  12 ounces quality bulk breakfast
    sausage, cooked, drained, and
    crumbled
  ¼ cup chopped fresh basil

ASSEMBLY
  2 Roma tomatoes, cut into
    ¼-inch slices
  4 ounces artichoke hearts,
    thinly sliced
  2 ounces seasoned or herbed
    Feta cheese
  4 scallions, finely chopped
    (reserve green tops for
    garnish)

Boil the potatoes until fork tender. Drain and let rest, uncovered. Add the butter; season with salt, pepper, and nutmeg. Mash potatoes with a fork or run them through a food processor until smooth. Add the egg yolks and combine. Keep the potatoes warm. Make the egg wash; set aside.

In a skillet, melt half the butter and lightly sauté the zucchini; set aside. In the same skillet, melt another tablespoon of the butter and sauté the red and yellow bell peppers until tender, just a few minutes.

Prepare the egg tarts. Combine the eggs and water and beat until smooth. Melt 1 tablespoon of butter in a 6-inch omelet pan. Add 3 ounces of the sausage and 1 tablespoon basil. Pour 4 ounces of the eggs into the pan and cook until set; turn over and cook on the other side. Remove and place on an ovenproof serving plate. Repeat for the other 3 servings. Keep warm.

Preheat the oven to 400°. When the tarts are cooked, add the tomato and artichoke slices in a circle, leaving about 1 inch of the outside of the cooked egg exposed. Spoon even amounts of peppers and zucchini in the center of each of the tarts; sprinkle the Feta cheese over the vegetables.

Insert a large star tip into a pastry bag and fill with the potato mixture. Pipe a border around the exposed outside edge of each tart. Brush with egg wash. Bake in the oven for 10 to 15 minutes, or until the potatoes are lightly browned. Garnish with the scallions.

Makes 4 servings

— *VICTORIAN TREASURE B&B*

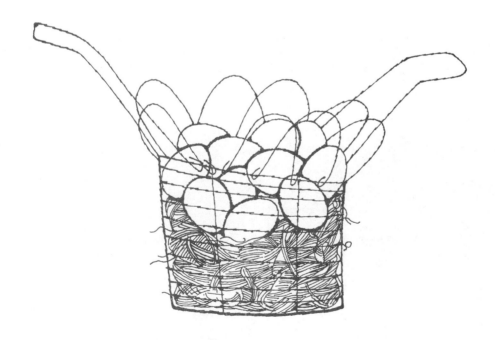

Ham-and-Cheese Egg Roll with Parsley Sauce

You may begin preparations for this dish a day ahead of time. The roll, or roulade, is made with eggs soufflé style and filled with ham and Swiss cheese, topped with a creamy parsley sauce.

SAUCE
- 1 cup Italian flat-leaf parsley leaves
- 2 shallots or 1 small onion
- 2 teaspoons dried basil or oregano
- 1½ cups whipping cream
- 1 tablespoon cornstarch
- 1 tablespoon Dijon-style mustard

EGG ROLL
- 6 egg yolks, beaten
- ¼ cup (½ stick) butter
- ½ cup all-purpose flour
- ⅛ teaspoon white pepper
- 2 cups milk
- 6 egg whites with ¼ teaspoon cream of tartar, beaten to stiff peaks

FILLING
- 6 ounces thinly sliced ham
- 6 ounces thinly sliced provolone cheese or Swiss cheese

Begin by making the sauce. Place all of the sauce ingredients into a food processor and process just until smooth. Do not overblend. In a 1½-quart saucepan, cook the mixture over medium heat until the sauce is thick and bubbly. Cook and stir for 1 more minute. Make ahead and store covered in the refrigerator.

Prepare the egg-roll base. Line a jelly-roll pan 10 x 15 inches with aluminum foil, extending the foil 1 inch beyond the edges. Grease and lightly flour the foil. Place the beaten egg yolks into a large mixing bowl.

Preheat the oven to 375°. In a 2-quart saucepan, melt the butter over medium-high heat; add the flour and pepper. Add the milk all at once, cooking and stirring until the mixture is thick and bubbly. Remove from the heat and slowly pour into the bowl with the beaten egg yolks. Fold a little of the egg whites into the yolk mixture to lighten, then repeat until all beaten whites are folded in.

Spread the mixture into the prepared pan. Bake for 20 minutes, or until puffed and lightly set. While the egg roll is baking, prepare another piece of foil, the size of the pan, and grease and flour it. When the egg roll is baked, immediately flip it over onto the new piece of foil and allow to cool at room temperature. When cool, place the filling ingredients evenly over the egg roll. Using the foil, roll the base up from the short side; place foil seam down on the baking sheet and refrigerate overnight.

When ready to bake, unwrap the egg roll and cut into 8 even pieces. Cover lightly with foil and bake at 375° for 40 minutes, or until the filling is thoroughly heated through. Warm the parsley sauce and serve.

Makes 8 servings

— *THE SOUTHERN HOTEL*

Island Eggs Benedict with Mango Salsa

Here it is, an Eggs Benedict even the most discriminating dieter can indulge in. Rather than the traditional rich Eggs Benedict with hollandaise sauce, here is a sauce made with sour cream (or substitute plain yogurt), and the eggs are served hard-boiled rather than soft-boiled. The refreshing mango salsa is optional, but you may want to have it on hand and serve it with other breakfast or lunch recipes or with crackers as an appetizer. Innkeeper Gloria Merkel taught us on camera to cut mangoes by first slicing the fruit away from the large pit in two slices. Then cut mango from the narrow edges (top and bottom) of the pit.

MANGO SALSA

- 2 large mangoes, peeled and cut into ¼-inch cubes
- 1 medium-sized cucumber, peeled, seeded, and cut into ¼-inch cubes
- 4 ounces roasted red peppers, drained and cut into ¼-inch cubes
- 1 medium red onion, cut into ¼-inch cubes
- ¼ cup chopped fresh cilantro or flat-leaf parsley
- 1½ tablespoons fresh lime juice
- 1½ tablespoons juice from pickled jalapeño peppers
- ⅛ teaspoon salt

EGGS

- 5 hard-boiled eggs
- 2 tablespoons butter
- 2 tablespoons all-purpose flour
- 1½ cups milk
- ½ cup sour cream
- 1 teaspoon Dijon-style mustard
- 1 cup shredded cheddar cheese
- 8 ounces fresh mushrooms
- 2 tablespoons butter
- 3 whole English muffins, cut into halves
- 18 large spinach leaves
- 6 tomato slices
- 6 slices quality ham or Canadian bacon
  Cilantro for garnish

Prepare the salsa. In a medium bowl, combine the mangoes, cucumber, red peppers, onion, cilantro, lime juice, pickled jalapeño juice, and the salt. Toss the ingredients gently but thoroughly. Let the salsa stand at room temperature for about 30 minutes to allow the flavors to meld. The salsa will make 3 cups, enough for 6 side servings with the Island Eggs Benedict.

Begin the Eggs Benedict. Shell the eggs and separate them. Dice the whites and crumble the yolks. In a medium saucepan over medium heat, melt the butter and stir in the flour, adding the milk slowly to form a roux. Stir until thickened. Add the sour cream, the mustard, and the cheese, stirring until blended.

Slice and sauté the mushrooms in the butter; add to the sour cream mixture with the egg whites. Remove from the heat and cover. Toast the muffins. Top each muffin with 3 spinach leaves, a slice of tomato, and a slice of ham. Before serving, warm assembled muffins in a microwave for just a few seconds. Top each with the sauce and garnish with the crumbled egg yolks and cilantro. Serve with a side dish of the Mango Salsa.

Makes 6 servings

— *GLORIA'S SPOUTING HORN B&B INN*

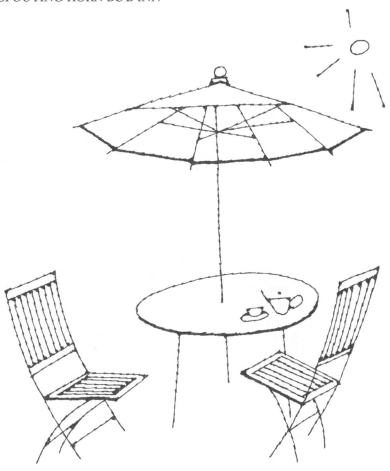

Cheese-and-Vegetable Filled Egg Blossom Crêpes

Thin batter crêpes fan out on a large muffin tin to resemble a big sunflower. Each "pod" is filled with eggs and vegetables, but you may add any combination you wish, including chopped sausage or bacon. The crêpe batter needs to rest for 1 hour before cooking.

CRÊPE BATTER
- 4 eggs
- ½ teaspoon salt
- 2 cups all-purpose flour
- 2½ cups milk
- ¼ cup butter, melted

FILLING
- 6 eggs
- 2 tablespoons all-purpose flour
- 1 cup half-and-half or light cream

- 1 (10-ounce) package frozen broccoli
- 2 cups shredded Cheddar cheese
- ½ teaspoon white pepper
- 3 tablespoons mayonnaise

GARNISH
- 6 to 8 large leaves of Savoy cabbage, kale, or any leafy curly green
- Edible flower petals (sunflower)

Combine all of the batter ingredients in a blender for about 1 minute, scraping down the sides of the blender. Refrigerate the batter for 1 hour. Spray a nonstick omelete pan. Pour a thin layer of batter into the pan and swirl to coat the bottom. Cook crêpe on each side until lightly browned. Set aside. Continue with remaining batter.

Preheat the oven to 350°. Generously coat a tin of 6 large-sized muffin cups with nonstick cooking oil spray. Place a crêpe in each of the cups, sprinkle with a little cheese, fanning the extra folds of the crêpe like flower petals around the outside of the cup. In a large bowl, combine the filling ingredients and pour evenly into each of the crêpe-lined muffin cups. Bake for 15 minutes. Cover with foil and bake for 15 minutes, or until golden and eggs are set.

Gently pry the crêpe cups from the pan and place each one in the center of a large green leaf. Garnish with shredded cheese and sunflower petals.

Makes 6 servings

— *THE WILDFLOWER INN*

French Toast and Waffles

Peaches-and-Cream-Stuffed Waffles with Praline Sauce

At the Ashley Inn, stuffed waffles are a breakfast signature. They stuff them with all sorts of combinations, and you will find a few of them on the next few pages. The inn uses a round waffle iron, which helps fold the waffles easily to stuff. If you are using a square or Belgian waffle iron, then fill as you would a sandwich, placing one waffle on top of the other.

BASIC WAFFLE MIX
  3 cups all-purpose flour
  2½ teaspoons baking powder
  ¼ teaspoon baking soda
  ¼ cup (½ stick) butter, melted
  ½ teaspoon salt
  4 eggs
  2 cups buttermilk

WAFFLE MIX ADD-ON
  2 teaspoons orange extract
  2 teaspoons grated orange rind

FILLING
12 ounces cream cheese,
      softened
½ cup powdered sugar

  1 teaspoon orange extract
  4 peaches, peeled and thinly
      sliced (reserve some for
      garnish)

SAUCE
  ½ cup (1 stick) butter
  2 cups lightly packed brown
      sugar
  1 cup whole pecans
  ½ cup water

GARNISH
      Sour cream
      Fresh mint sprigs
      Peach slices

Combine the waffle-batter ingredients, mixing just until smooth. Stir in the waffle-mix add-ons of orange extract and orange rind. Set aside. Preheat the waffle iron, coating with a nonstick spray. While the iron heats, combine the filling ingredients except for the peaches, mixing until smooth. Heat in a small saucepan until the sugar is completely dissolved. Remove from heat and set aside.

Make your waffles and spread about 3 tablespoons of the filling on each waffle. Add a layer of the peaches and fold the top of each waffle over. Blanket with the warm praline sauce and garnish with a dollop of sour cream, a peach slice, and a sprig of mint.

Makes 8 waffles

— *THE ASHLEY INN*

Sausage-and-Cheese-Stuffed Herb Waffles

While this is a fabulous breakfast entrée, it is also satisfying for lunch or a light dinner.
Basic Waffle Mix (page 35)

FILLING
1 medium onion, finely chopped
2 tablespoons finely chopped green bell pepper
1 pound bulk sausage, cooked and drained
1 cup grated cheddar cheese
½ cup cottage cheese

BASIC BATTER ADD-ONS
1 teaspoon finely chopped fresh sage
½ teaspoon fennel seeds
½ teaspoon finely chopped fresh thyme
½ cup finely chopped pecans (optional)

SAUCE
2 eggs
6 tablespoons lemon juice
½ teaspoon salt
1 cup (2 sticks) butter

GARNISH
Fresh sage leaves
Fresh sprigs of thyme

In a large skillet, sauté the onion and pepper until soft. Mix in the cooked sausage and the cheeses. Keep warm.

Preheat the waffle iron and prepare the basic batter as described on page 36, mixing in the add-ons listed here of sage, fennel seeds, thyme, and optional pecans.

While preparing the waffles, make the sauce. Combine the eggs, lemon juice, and salt in a blender. In a small pan, melt the butter until bubbling. Turn on the blender and, while processing, pour in the butter and blend until thickened. Pour the mixture into a small pan and keep over hot water until ready to use. Make the waffles.

Place about ½ cup of the filling onto each waffle. Fold the top over and serve with the sauce. Garnish with fresh herbs.

Makes 8 servings

— *THE ASHLEY INN*

Blueberry-Cheese-and-Lemon-Stuffed Waffles

*Drained ricotta cheese and sweet berries tinged with an essence of lemon
make this waffle breakfast a winner. Use the Basic Waffle Mix on page 35.
The ricotta needs to drain, so start this recipe about 3 hours ahead of
serving time, or strain overnight in the refrigerator.*

FILLING
12 ounces ricotta cheese
½ cup powdered sugar
 1 cup fresh or frozen blueberries
 1 teaspoon lemon extract

BASIC BATTER ADD-ONS
 2 teaspoons lemon extract
 2 teaspoons grated lemon rind

SAUCE
 2 cups fresh blueberries, or
   frozen, thawed and well-
   drained
 1 cup sugar
 1 cup water
 2 tablespoons orange liqueur
 2 tablespoons cornstarch
½ cup water

GARNISH
   Powdered sugar for dusting
   Vanilla or plain yogurt
   Lemon twist or mint
   Mint sprigs

Begin by preparing the filling. Place the ricotta in a strainer or cheesecloth over a bowl to drain for about 2 to 3 hours. When drained, mix
the ricotta in a bowl with the powdered sugar, blueberries, and lemon
extract. Set aside.

Preheat the waffle iron and prepare the basic batter as described on
page 36, including the waffle-batter add-ons for this recipe of the
lemon extract and grated lemon rind. Make the waffles.

While the waffles bake, prepare the sauce. Place the berries,
sugar, and water in a small saucepan. Bring to a boil and add the
liqueur. Dissolve the cornstarch in the water and add to the berries.
Cook over moderate heat until the sauce is glassy in appearance and
not too thick.

To assemble, spread 4 tablespoons of filling on each waffle and
fold over. Dust with powdered sugar and top with the sauce. Garnish
with a dollop of yogurt and a sprig of mint.

Makes 8 servings

— *THE ASHLEY INN*

Raspberries-and-Cream French Toast with Spiced Peach Sauce

The jewel-tone colors in this lush stove-top breakfast dish complement the inn's Victorian period. All around Victorian Treasure, period artifacts glow like fresh juicy fruit. You will want to make this dish for company. It is splendid and evocative of happy times. Enjoy!

SAUCE
1½ pounds ripe fresh peaches
2 tablespoons butter
⅓ cup brown sugar
1 cup canned cling peaches in syrup
⅓ cup water
⅓ cup corn syrup
1 tablespoon vanilla extract
½ teaspoon ground cinnamon
¼ teaspoon grated nutmeg
¼ teaspoon ground cloves

FILLING
1 loaf Vienna-style (Italian) bread
8 ounces cream cheese, softened
½ cup raspberry pie filling

BATTER
4 eggs
2 cups whole milk or cream
1 tablespoon vanilla extract
¼ teaspoon ground cinnamon
¼ cup (½ stick) butter, melted

GARNISH
½ pint fresh raspberries

Peel half of the fresh peaches. (To peel peaches, roll the peach using a skewer or fork in simmering water until softened. Cool on a towel. Peel with a vegetable peeler.) Cut peeled peaches into 1-inch chunks. Set aside. Cut the remaining fresh peaches, skin on, into 12 to 16 thin slices. Set aside. Meanwhile, prepare the French toast.

Melt the butter in a saucepan over medium-high heat. Add the brown sugar, stirring until melted. Add the fresh peach chunks and sauté for several minutes, until the peaches are soft. Meanwhile, in a food processor, purée the cling peaches; add them to the sauce. Add water, corn syrup, vanilla, and the spices. Cook the mixture for 10 to 15 minutes, or until the peaches are tender. Add the remaining sliced peaches to the sauce about 5 minutes before sauce finishing time.

Cut 8 slices of bread, approximately 1½ inches thick. Cut a pocket from the top of the slice down through the middle without cutting in half.

Gently swirl the raspberry pie filling into the cream cheese; do not overmix. Spoon 2 tablespoons of the cream cheese mixture into each bread pocket.

In a mixing bowl, beat together the eggs, milk, vanilla, and cinnamon, just until incorporated.

Heat a griddle and add enough of the butter to cover the griddle. Dip each stuffed bread slice into egg batter and sauté until golden brown, adding more butter to sauté as needed.

Remove the bread from the griddle; slice diagonally. Place on the plate, overlapping the slices. Ladle hot spiced peach sauce over the top. Garnish with fresh raspberries.

Makes 8 servings

— *VICTORIAN TREASURE B & B INN*

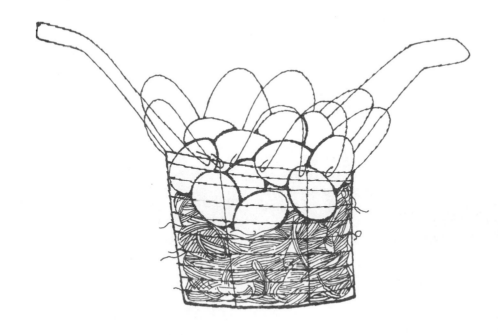

Morning Cakes

Rose Petal Muffins

Made with edible rose petals, these fragrant muffins are dense and very filling. Make them in a special cast-iron flowerpot pan to create a floral shape, or bake in glazed flowerpots. Serve with Rose Flower Jelly on page 145. (If using the Flower-Scented Sugar in this recipe, you will need to make it first, a few weeks ahead of the muffins.) Innkeeper Donna Stone credits The Herb Farm in Fredericksburg, Texas, for her inspiration.

1½ cups all-purpose flour
2 teaspoons baking powder
¼ cup (½ stick) butter
½ cup Flower-Scented Sugar (page 144)

½ teaspoon salt
¼ cup edible rose petals
1 egg
½ cup milk
¼ teaspoon vanilla extract

Preheat the oven to 400°. Sift together the flour and baking powder in a large bowl. Cut the butter into the flour mixture with a pastry blender. Set aside. Mix the sugar and salt with the rose petals and add it to the flour mixture. Add the egg, milk, and vanilla and mix just until blended. Batter will be stiff.

Coat the cast-iron flowerpot pans or the flowerpots with a nonstick cooking oil spray. Place in the oven and bake for 20 minutes, or until a tester comes clean. Serve with Rose Flower Jelly page 145.

Makes 4 muffins

— THE WILDFLOWER INN

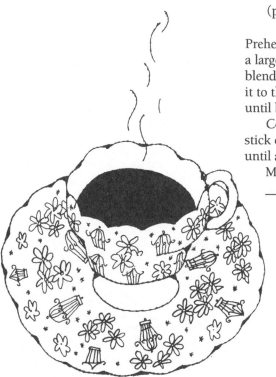

Oat-Crusted Galettes with Cranberry-Apricot Filling

Innkeeper Laura Simoes loves to talk shop with Ken Headrich, a New England cookbook author from whom Laura sometimes draws her breakfast inspiration, as in this recipe from Simple Desserts *(Bantam 1995). Ken calls these luscious tartlike desserts crostadas, as the crust is free-form and then pleated around the fruit; they're also known as galettes.*

CRUST
- ⅓ cup rolled old-fashioned oats
- 2 tablespoons sugar
- ⅛ teaspoon salt
- 1¼ cups all-purpose flour
- ½ cup (1 stick) very cold unsalted butter, cut into 1¼-inch slices
- 1 egg yolk
- 2 tablespoons cold water

FILLING
- 4 tablespoons apricot preserves
- ½ cup fresh cranberries
- ¼ cup sugar
- 8 ripe fresh apricots

Begin with the crust. Put the oats, sugar, and salt in a food processor and process to a fine meal, about 30 to 40 seconds. Add the flour and process for 8 seconds more. Add the butter and process for about 8 seconds, or until the butter is broken into very small pieces. Stir the egg yolk and water in a small bowl. Sprinkle this egg mixture over the oats-and-flour mixture and process for 4 seconds. Fluff up the ingredients with a fork and process for about another 4 seconds, until the pastry just starts to gather into a mass.

Turn the pastry out onto a work surface and pack it into a ball. If it does not pack easily, sprinkle a teaspoon of water over the dry areas and quickly work it in with your fingertips. Knead the dough twice. Flatten the dough into a disk about 3/4 inch thick and refrigerate for 30 to 45 minutes. (Do not let the dough get rock-hard.) When the dough is firm but not too hard, roll it into a 13- to 14-inch circle on a sheet of lightly floured waxed paper. Invert the pastry onto a baking sheet and remove the paper.

Preheat the oven to 425°. Melt the preserves over low heat. Combine the cranberries and sugar in the bowl of a food processor and set aside. Cut each apricot into halves and remove the pit. Then cut each half into thirds. Spread the melted preserves over the pastry round. Top the preserves with the cranberry-and-sugar mixture, spreading it over the pastry. Arrange the sliced apricots in a decorative pattern over the top, leaving a 1⅓-inch border around the outside. Fold up the edges and pleat the dough to make the crostada, or galette. (The preserves will show through the center.) Bake for 20 minutes, then lower the heat to 400° and bake for another 30 minutes, until the galette is brown and the filling is a little bubbly. Cool on the pan for another 15 to 20 minutes before slicing into wedges.

Note: Here is Ken Headrich's variation with a different filling: Apple Honey Crostada Filling:

Fill the dough with a mixture of 3 tablespoons raw honey; 2 teaspoons cinnamon; 4 large Granny Smith apples, peeled, cored, and chopped into bite-size pieces; ¾ cup mixture of golden and dark raisins. Proceed as for the crostada pastry, but spread with the honey; sprinkle on the cinnamon, apples, and raisins. Bake as directed.

Makes 6 servings

— *THE INN AT MAPLEWOOD FARM*

Old-Fashioned Fresh-Fruit Coffee Cake with Streusel Topping

The warm morning sun was radiating on the inn's front porch, reflecting light through the cake to the glistening fruit underneath. Such was my first taste of Todd Seidl's delicious cake. This is the result of the time innkeeper Todd and wife Kimberly spend together cooking in the kitchen. This is one couple whose love in the kitchen is an added bonus to guests in the dining room. Add fresh fruits in season such as plums, nectarines, apples. Lemon or maple syrup may be added to the icing for flavor, and you may sprinkle nuts over the top of the cake before baking.

TOPPING
⅓ cup all-purpose flour
½ cup sugar
¼ cup butter, softened

BATTER
1 cup all-purpose flour
½ cup sugar
2 teaspoons baking powder
½ teaspoon salt
2 tablespoons butter, melted
½ cup milk
1 egg
1 teaspoon vanilla extract
2 cups fresh-fruit mix such as strawberries, blueberries, rasp-berries, rhubarb

ICING
½ cup powdered sugar
2 teaspoons hot milk
¼ teaspoon vanilla extract

First, make the streusel topping. In a medium bowl, mix together the flour, sugar, and butter until the mixture resembles coarse crumbs. Set aside.

Preheat the oven to 375°. Prepare the batter. In a large bowl, mix together the flour, sugar, baking powder, and salt. Set aside. Melt the butter and let cool. In a mixing bowl, whip the butter with the milk, the egg, and the vanilla. Add the butter-egg mixture to the bowl of dry ingredients. Stir just until blended. Pour into a greased 8-inch spring-form pan. Top with the fruit, fanning the fruit around the batter. Follow with the streusel, adding the topping evenly around the cake.

Bake for 35 to 40 minutes or until the top of the cake is lightly browned. Remove the cake from the oven and let cool. Mix the icing ingredients together in a large bowl. When cooled, remove the sides of the pan and cut the cake into wedges to serve. Drizzle with icing.

Makes 8 servings

— *VICTORIAN TREASURE B & B INN*

Coffee-Glazed Cake Cubes with Macadamia Nut Crusts

An on-the-run food that has the flavor of coffee and the depth of those wonderful Hawaiian nuts, these are great on a brunch buffet table or packed as a snack for a morning picnic.

⅔ cup sugar, plus ¼ cup sugar
⅓ cup quality brewed coffee
1 teaspoon instant espresso powder
¼ cup Kahlúa or other coffee-based liqueur

1 cup toasted macadamia nuts, finely ground
1 plain or chocolate-swirl pound cake, cut into 1-inch cubes

In a small saucepan, combine the ⅔ cup of sugar with the brewed coffee and the espresso powder. Stir the mixture over medium heat to dissolve the sugar. Bring the mixture to a boil and keep boiling for 1 minute. Remove the saucepan from the heat and cool for 1 minute. Stir in the Kahlúa. Pour the mixture into a small bowl, cooling it completely.

In another small bowl, combine the nuts and the remaining ¼ cup sugar. Dip each pound cake cube into the cooled coffee syrup and then roll in the nut-and-sugar mixture to coat completely. Allow to dry on racks for about 2 hours before serving.

Makes 3 dozen

— *THE SOUTHERN HOTEL*

Herbed
Focaccia Bread

ALL IN AN AFTERNOON

Salads, Sandwiches, Tea-Time Sweets

Salads

Citrus and Roasted Red Pepper Salad with Balsamic Vinaigrette

The colors of this salad rival the brilliance of those on the Italian flag itself. Simple to make, serve this with a soup and crusty bread for lunch or as an antipasto for dinner. To roast a red pepper, simply blacken the pepper in a hot oven or over an open fire. To make the garlic paste, pulverize 2 fresh garlic cloves with a knife. Garlic paste allows the flavor of garlic to permeate the dish as opposed to getting bits of garlic to bite into.

1 small head romaine lettuce
1 small head red-leaf lettuce
1 large orange, peeled and sliced very thin
1 large sweet red bell pepper, roasted, peeled, seeded, and sliced very thin
½ cup green olives (the kind packed in oil), drained

¼ cup extra-virgin olive oil
4 tablespoons quality balsamic vinegar
1 teaspoon garlic paste
2 tablespoons fresh minced basil
Fresh ground pepper and salt

Tear the lettuces into bite-size pieces. Place into a large salad bowl and add the orange slices, red pepper, and olives. Set aside.

In a lidded jar, mix together the olive oil, vinegar, garlic paste, and basil. Shake the bottle and pour over the salad. Toss gently. Add salt and pepper to taste.

Makes 6 servings

— THE CAPTAIN FREEMAN INN

Roasted Red Pepper and Fennel Salad

When the fennel bulb is roasted, it spreads into a clawlike pattern reminiscent of the black bears that sometimes visit the inn during the early summer mornings. I think they just smell Chef Scott Parker's intoxicating cuisine so they are drawn to the inn for something to eat and a good night's sleep, and in the morning they know breakfast is on the buffet. But only to dream. Poor bears!

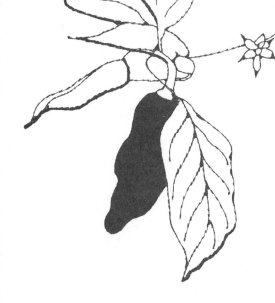

1 medium onion
1 cup extra-virgin olive oil
1 fennel bulb, fronds and ribs discarded
½ cup balsamic vinegar
1 teaspoon minced garlic
1 teaspoon sugar

1 teaspoon dry mustard
5 ounces field greens, washed and dried
2 medium red bell peppers, roasted
Salt and pepper

Preheat the oven to 450°. Rub the onion with some of the olive oil. Place in the oven and roast the onion, turning occasionally until the onion is brown on all sides, about 20 minutes. Remove from the oven, set aside and cool. Turn the oven down to 300°.

Halve the fennel bulb and cut it into thin slices so that some core is attached to each slice. Rub the slices with oil and lay them flat on a baking sheet. Place in the oven and roast until browned, about 10 to 15 minutes. Remove from the oven and set aside to cool.

In a medium mixing bowl, combine the vinegar, garlic, sugar, and mustard. Slowly add the remaining oil in a thin stream while mixing continuously with a whisk to emulsify. Season to taste. Toss the greens with the vinaigrette. Peel the onion and cut into julienne. Seed and dice the peppers. Mix the onion and peppers in with the greens. Divide among 4 plates and garnish with the roasted fennel bulb slices. Season with salt and pepper to taste.

Makes 4 servings

— SAN SOPHIA INN

Pecan and Romaine Salad with Sweet-and-Sour Dressing

Simple, bursting with flavor and the crunch of Mississippi's fresh pecans, this is a salad that goes with most any meal.

1 large head romaine lettuce
4 or 5 green onions, bottom and tops, finely chopped
2 cups steamed asparagus tips
1 cup very small or coarsely chopped pecans
2 tablespoons butter

DRESSING
1 cup salad oil
¼ cup soy sauce
½ cup red-wine vinegar
¾ cup sugar

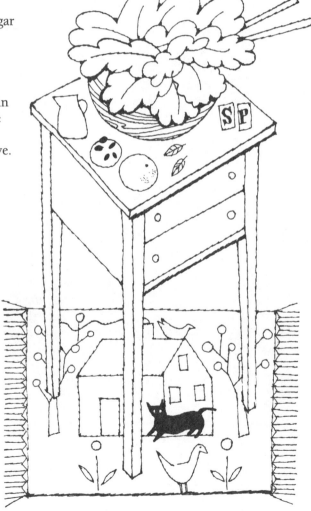

Wash the lettuce leaves, pat dry, and tear into pieces. Mix in a bowl with the onions and asparagus tips. Set aside. Sauté the pecans in the butter until golden. Add to the salad.

Add the dressing ingredients to the bowl and toss. Serve.
Makes 8 servings

— *THE CEDARS PLANTATION*

Warm Spinach Salad with Nectarine Vinaigrette

San Sophia Inn, set amidst the San Juan Mountains, offers fine dining and après ski with a menu that boasts Little Foods and Big Foods. In the mood for serving your own guests something fresh and tingly? Serve this salad with a fruity sparkling wine such as Domaine Carneros Brut. Chef Scott Parker does not spare the butter, but the recipe is still delicious with half the suggested amount.

VINEGAR
1 cup white-wine vinegar
2 nectarines, coarsely chopped

SALAD
1 pound fresh spinach leaves, stems removed
1 cup (2 sticks) butter
1 shallot, minced
3 nectarines, halved and cut into thin slices, plus 1 sliced nectarine for garnish
1 tablespoon sugar
Salt and pepper

Combine the vinegar and the chopped nectarines in a small saucepan and cook over very low heat for about 2 hours, or until the fruit is softened and combined. Keep warm.

When the vinaigrette is done, prepare the salad. Tear the spinach into bite-size pieces. Heat a small sauté pan and add 1 tablespoon of the butter. Sauté the shallot in the butter until softened. Add the vinegar and the sugar and cook over moderate heat until reduced to half. Add the nectarines and the remaining butter. Stir with a whisk to emulsify. Season with salt and pepper.

In a large salad bowl, toss the spinach with the warm vinaigrette. Spinach should wilt slightly. Divide into 4 portions and garnish with nectarine slices.

Makes 4 servings

— *SAN SOPHIA INN*

Wilted Salad with Walnuts, Pear, Stilton, and Orange Vinaigrette

The gentle combination of pear with orange contrasted by the Stilton cheese provides a most satisfying dish for lunch or as a prelude to dinner. Chef Scott Parker even recommends this as an after-dinner course.

SALAD
5 ounces mixed field greens
½ cup chopped walnuts
1 pear
1 tablespoon butter
1 tablespoon brown sugar
¼ teaspoon salt

DRESSING
Grated rind of 1 orange
Juice from 1 orange
1 egg yolk
2 tablespoons red-wine vinegar
1 tablespoon orange liqueur
1 tablespoon sugar
1 tablespoon salt
White pepper to taste
1 cup salad oil

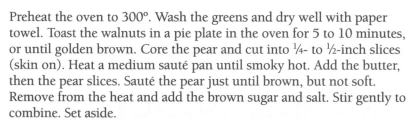

ASSEMBLY
2 ounces Stilton or blue cheese

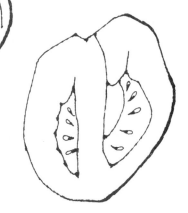

Preheat the oven to 300°. Wash the greens and dry well with paper towel. Toast the walnuts in a pie plate in the oven for 5 to 10 minutes, or until golden brown. Core the pear and cut into ¼- to ½-inch slices (skin on). Heat a medium sauté pan until smoky hot. Add the butter, then the pear slices. Sauté the pear just until brown, but not soft. Remove from the heat and add the brown sugar and salt. Stir gently to combine. Set aside.

Prepare the dressing. In a medium nonreactive bowl, combine the orange rind, juice, and egg yolk. Mix well. Add all of the other ingredients except for the oil. Transfer the mixture to the top of a double boiler. Over gently simmering water, whip the mixture until slightly thickened. Be careful not to get the mixture too hot or the egg will curdle. Remove from the heat and slowly add the oil in a thin stream. Whip to emulsify.

Toss the greens in a large bowl, adding the dressing. Divide among the serving plates and add the pears and walnuts. Garnish with crumbles of the Stilton cheese.

Makes 4 servings

— SAN SOPHIA INN

Shrimp-Papaya Salad in Avocado with Mango-Macadamia Dressing

This clean, flavorful California dish makes a perfect salad for a hot summer's night or a midwinter lunch when you're longing for a literal taste of the Tropics. Chef Joan Dawkins teaches us here that you can actually squeeze juice out of a mango.

SALAD
 3 ripe avocados, peeled, stone removed, and cut into halves
   Juice of 1 lemon
 3 ripe papayas, peeled and seeded
 ½ cup thinly sliced onion
 2 pounds cooked medium shrimp, cut lengthwise into halves
 1 large bunch fresh watercress (about 1½ cups)

DRESSING
 2 very ripe medium-sized mangoes
 1 ripe avocado, peeled, stone removed, and cut into chunks
 2 teaspoons lemon juice
 2 tablespoons dry vermouth
 2 tablespoons chopped fresh mint
   Freshly ground pepper
 ½ cup extra-virgin olive oil

GARNISHES
   Finely grated rind of 1 lemon
 2 heads Belgian endive
 ½ cup toasted and crushed macadamia nuts

Place the peeled avocado halves in the lemon juice and drain. Fill the avocado with the papaya, onion, and the shrimp. Top with the watercress. Set aside and make the dressing.

Cut off the ends of the mango and squeeze out as much juice of the mango as possible into a small mixing bowl. In a food processor, blend the avocado with the lemon juice until creamy. Add to the mango juice. Add the vermouth, the mint, and a taste of pepper. Pour in the olive oil, blending all of the ingredients.

Drizzle the dressing evenly over the stuffed avocado. Garnish with lemon rind, a leaf of endive, and a sprinkling of the nuts.

Makes 6 servings

— ORCHARD HILL COUNTRY INN

Broccoli Noodle Salad

A picnic is not complete without this delicious and nutritious salad that is also great looking. Here is a perfect opportunity to try soba noodles without being intimidated. The inn sends guests off with such filling dishes as this one as they go off to explore the surrounding streams and mountain paths.

SALAD

- 6 ounces Japanese soba noodles or angel hair pasta
- 3 tablespoons sesame oil, divided
- 1 bunch broccoli florets and stems
- 1 cup thinly sliced red cabbage
- 1 cup packed coarsely grated carrots
- ½ cup thinly sliced green onion
- ½ cup sliced almonds, toasted

DRESSING

- ¼ cup vegetable oil
- ⅓ cup rice vinegar
- 3 tablespoons soy sauce
- 2 teaspoons minced fresh ginger
- 1 clove garlic, minced
  A few drops hot chili oil

Cook the noodles as per package instructions. Drain, rinse, and toss with 1 tablespoon of the sesame oil. Set aside.

Cut broccoli florets into bite-size pieces. Lightly blanch in boiling salted water. Drain, then run under cold water to stop the cooking process. Drain again. Peel and thinly slice the broccoli stems. Combine the stems, florets, cabbage, carrots, onions, and almonds in a nonreactive container.

Combine the vegetable oil, rice vinegar, the remaining sesame oil, soy sauce, fresh ginger, garlic, and chili oil. Mix well. Add noodles and dressing to the vegetable mixture, mixing well. Taste and adjust seasonings.

Makes 6 to 8 servings

— THE STEAMBOAT INN

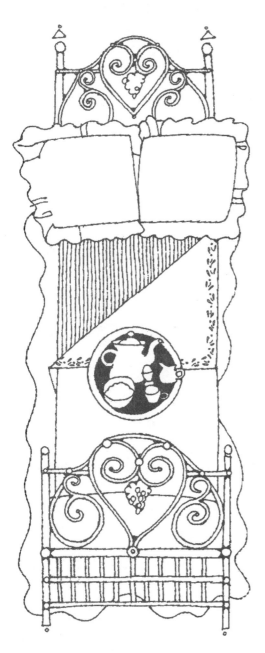

Sandwiches

Fig and Mango Pork Quesadillas

The variations in texture and flavor in this open-faced quesadilla, better known as a tostada, are most innovative. Do not let the long list of ingredients dissuade you; they all go into a mixture at once. The recipe takes little time to prepare. Great served for lunch with a garden salad.

8 tablespoons butter, separated
6 8-inch flour tortillas
¼ cup all-purpose flour
1 pound pork tenderloin, cut into small dice
2 tablespoons butter, melted
¼ cup finely diced yellow bell pepper
¼ cup finely diced red bell pepper
¼ cup diced red onion
1 tablespoon Anaheim chilies, minced
1 teaspoon minced garlic
1 teaspoon cumin
1 teaspoon chili powder
1 teaspoon oregano
1 teaspoon finely chopped fresh basil
1 teaspoon finely chopped fresh cilantro
½ cup peeled and finely diced mango
½ cup finely diced **mission** figs
½ cup skinned, seeded, and finely diced tomatoes
1½ cups Monterey Jack cheese, shredded

Preheat the oven to 350°. In a nonstick 10-inch sauté pan, melt 1 tablespoon of the butter over medium heat. Place a tortilla in the pan and sauté until golden brown on both sides. (It helps to use tongs to turn tortillas.) Remove the tortilla from the pan and place on a paper towel to remove any excess butter. Repeat with remaining tortillas. Place the tortillas on a large ungreased sheet pan; set aside.

Place the flour in a large plastic bag. Add the pork to the bag and fasten the bag at the top. Shake until the meat is lightly coated; remove from the bag and shake off any excess flour. Add the 2 remaining tablespoons of butter to a medium sauté pan and cook the pork over medium heat until browned, about 4 to 5 minutes. Add the

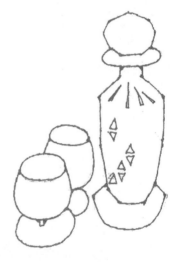

onion, bell peppers, chilies, garlic, cumin, chili powder, oregano, basil, and cilantro to the pork. Sauté for 3 to 4 minutes, or until the vegetables are tender. If the mixture begins to stick, add a little water to the pan. Gradually add the mango, figs, and tomatoes, cooking for an additional 3 to 4 minutes. Remove from the heat and place in a large bowl; mix thoroughly.

Place equal amounts of the mixture onto each tortilla, topping with about 4 tablespoons each of the cheese. Bake for 6 to 7 minutes or until the cheese is melted. Remove from the oven and serve.

Makes 6 servings

— *INN AT OLDE NEW BERLIN*

Maple-Glazed Leek, Brie, and Ham Sandwiches

Although this is in the lunch section of the cookbook, they make these delightful light and very tasty sandwiches at the inn for breakfast. Serve with a salad for lunch, but for breakfast serve with a side order of eggs.

2 tablespoons unsalted butter, plus more for griddle
2 large or 3 small leeks, green tops included, sliced lengthwise
3 tablespoons maple syrup
⅓ cup water
8 slices raisin bread or hearty wheat bread
4 ounces Brie cheese, thinly sliced
4 slices quality breakfast ham

In a medium-sized frying pan, melt the 2 tablespoons of unsalted butter. Chop the leeks coarsely and add them to the pan. Sauté until nearly soft, several minutes. Add the maple syrup and water. Simmer, uncovered, for 5 to 8 minutes, or until the leeks are soft. Set aside. Make 4 sandwiches with the Brie and ham, evenly divided. Top each sandwich with a portion of the maple-glazed leeks and cover each with a remaining slice of bread. Melt some additional butter on a griddle. Fry each sandwich on both sides until golden in color and the cheese is melted. Cut each sandwich diagonally into halves and serve.

Makes 4 servings

— *THE INN AT MAPLEWOOD FARM*

Crescent Moon and Star Meat Pasties

Medieval food was often made into shapes, especially inspired by the universe, hence meat pasties or small meat pies have been popular for a long time. In England, they maintain these traditions by selling pasties in bakeries. At Ravenwood Castle, Chef Deb Coyan serves these with many meals that are served in the Middle Ages style. She would have made Merlin proud every time.

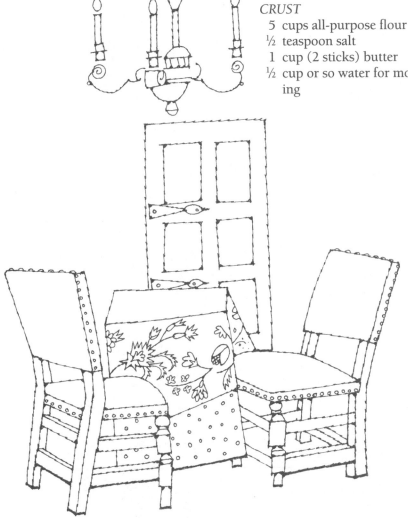

CRUST
  5 cups all-purpose flour
  ½ teaspoon salt
  1 cup (2 sticks) butter
  ½ cup or so water for moistening

FILLING
  1½ cups heavy white sauce (substitute 1 regular can cream of chicken soup)
  1½ cups cooked diced (small) chicken
  1½ cups white potatoes, boiled and cut into small dice
  1 teaspoon dried thyme
  ½ teaspoon salt

ASSEMBLY
  Heavy cream or half-and-half for glazing

Preheat the oven to 375°. In a medium-sized bowl, spoon in the flour and salt and cut in the butter. Add enough water to make a pliable dough. Roll the dough out to ⅛- to ¼-inch thin. Using a 6-inch dish and a knife, cut out 8 rounds of dough. (Save the pastry scraps.) Set aside.

Mix the filling ingredients in a bowl and evenly divide the filling among the rounds, placing the filling so that you can fold the dough over to form a crescent moon shape. Seal the edges firmly with water.

Using pastry scraps, cut out 8 small stars with a cookie cutter. Rub a drop of water on the back of the star to make it adhere to the pastry. Rub the entire top of each crescent with heavy cream or half-and-half to give it a brown glaze. Make a few very small holes to allow the steam to escape. Bake on nonstick cookie sheets for about 45 minutes or until golden brown.

Makes 8 servings

— *RAVENWOOD CASTLE*

Creamed Chicken in Cornbread Cups

You cannot go wrong with this splendid southern dish made the inn's way with cornbread cups. You may also serve the recipe on toast points or in puff pastry shells.

CORNBREAD CUPS
8 ounces cream cheese
1½ cups all-purpose flour
¾ cup yellow cornmeal
½ teaspoon salt

CHICKEN
3½ pounds chicken breasts,
  bones and skins intact
3 cups highly seasoned chicken
  broth
1 peeled whole onion, cut into
  halves
2 green bell peppers, one of
  them finely chopped, the
  other cut into bite-size pieces
1 rib celery, cut into halves
2 carrots, cut into large pieces
  Salt and pepper to taste
3 sprigs rosemary
1 tablespoon plus ½ cup
  (1 stick) butter
6 tablespoons all-purpose flour
¾ cup sliced water chestnuts
½ cup slivered almonds, toasted
4 ounces canned mushrooms,
  sliced
½ cup chopped pimentos

Mix the ingredients for the cornbread cups in a food processor, whirling just until a ball is formed. Remove the dough from the processor and knead briefly, just enough to create a smooth dough. Cover in plastic wrap and place in the refrigerator for 1 hour.

Meanwhile, prepare the chicken. Place the chicken in a Dutch oven and stew with the chicken broth, the onion, the finely chopped green pepper, celery, carrots, a sprinkling of salt and pepper, and rosemary sprigs. Simmer over medium-low heat for 45 minutes to 1 hour, or until the chicken is tender. Remove the chicken from the

pan and remove the meat from the bones. Cut the chicken into bite-size pieces; strain the broth, discard the vegetables, skim the fat, and reserve broth.

Heat the 1 tablespoon of butter in a sauté pan and sauté the remaining bell pepper. Add to the chicken. Set aside.

Prepare a sauce for the chicken by melting the ½ cup of butter in a large saucepan. Add the flour and the reserved chicken broth. Cook over medium-high heat, stirring frequently until thickened. Add the chicken, water chestnuts, almonds, and mushrooms. Set aside, keeping warm.

Preheat the oven to 350°. Remove the muffin cup batter from the refrigerator and evenly line 10 to 12 greased muffin cups with the batter. Bake in the oven for 20 to 30 minutes, or until golden. Watch carefully. Fill the cups with the warmed creamed chicken. Garnish with pimentos and serve.

Makes 10 to 12 servings

— *THE CEDARS PLANTATION*

Turkey Croissant Sandwiches with Cranberry Relish

I make a version of this sandwich by using fresh turkey and no chicken stock and cranberry sauce, rather than making the relish. But this relish is so good that I have kept it handy in my pantry now instead of using the cranberry sauce. I also add alfalfa sprouts. During the TV show, we took this delightful inn sandwich with us on a scenic picnic. I hope you were there. If not, at least here we can give you a taste.

6 croissants (the inn uses honey-wheat croissants)

1 recipe for Cranberry Relish (see page 141)

2 cups chicken stock

12 ounces thinly sliced quality cooked turkey

6 thin slices quality Swiss cheese

Slice the croissants lengthwise. Warm the relish and heat the chicken stock in a shallow skillet. Add the turkey to the skillet and heat in the chicken stock to keep the turkey from drying out.

To assemble, spoon a generous tablespoon of the relish on the bottom half of each croissant. Top with 2 ounces of turkey, a slice of cheese, and top with the other half of the croissant.

If desired, place in the oven just long enough to melt the cheese. Remove from the oven and top each sandwich with an additional dollop of the relish.

Makes 6 servings

— *THE STEAMBOAT INN*

Tea-Time Sweets

Tea Latte

While coffee is all the rage in its many forms, tea latte is coming into vogue. Although it is centuries-old, tea latte (known as Chai) made its debut on Country Inn Cooking with Gail Greco *only recently. Innkeeper Laura Simoes showed us how to put this refreshing drink together.*

1 quart whole milk	⅓ cup honey
1 teaspoon ground cinnamon	1 quart water
½ teaspoon ground cardamom	8 teaspoons loose orange pekoe
1 teaspoon ground almonds	or other black tea

In a large saucepan, combine the milk, cinnamon, cardamom, and almonds. Simmer for ½ hour, stirring occasionally. Add the honey and then immediately remove the brew from the heat. In a separate saucepan, boil the 1 quart of water. Pour the boiling water into a teapot with the tea. Steep for 5 minutes. Add the hot milk mixture to the tea in a ration of 1 to 1. Pour back and forth between the 2 containers to mix. Return the mixture to the teapot and strain before serving.

Makes 6 to 8 servings

— *THE INN AT MAPLEWOOD FARM*

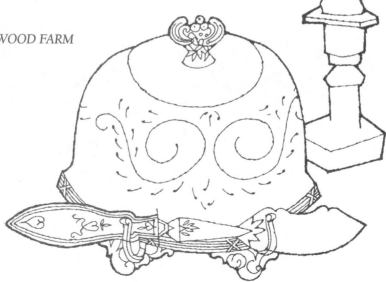

Spirited Chocolate Drink

This delightful beverage is especially nice after dinner. First, you will have a lot of laughs, and then you will sleep peacefully and contentedly.

3 cups ice cubes
1 ounce vodka
1 ounce Kahlúa

1 ounce Bailey's Irish Cream
2 scoops chocolate ice cream
Whipped cream for garnish

Mix together above ingredients in a food processor. Blend until smooth and serve with a dollop of whipped cream.

Makes 2 servings

— THE INN AT MAPLEWOOD FARM

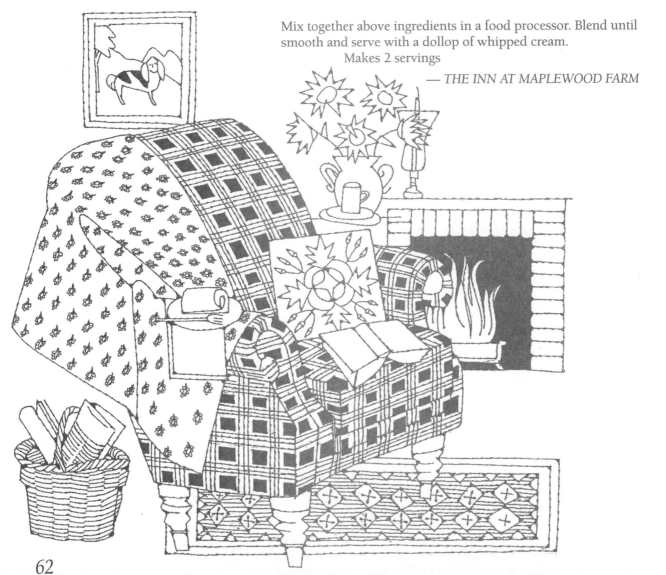

Oatmeal Tea Cake with Coconut-Pecan Frosting

When it is tea-time in the Tetons, innkeeper Kay Minns cooks up a variety of goodies for the table, including her grandmother's home-on-the-range cake that she shared with us on television. This is an easy and delightful cake that you can always count on to get raves as Kay does while guests sip tea after a day in the Grand Teton Mountain Range.

CAKE
1⅓ cups boiling water
 1 cup quick-cooking oatmeal
    flakes
 ½ cup (1 stick) butter
 1 cup brown sugar
 2 eggs
1½ cups all-purpose flour
 ½ teaspoon baking soda
 1 teaspoon ground cinnamon
 ½ teaspoon salt

FROSTING
 1 cup coarsely chopped pecans
 ½ cup whipping cream
 1 teaspoon vanilla extract
 1 cup unsweetened coconut
 1 cup brown sugar
 ¼ cup (½ stick) butter

Preheat the oven to 350°. Pour the boiling water over the oatmeal and let stand for 20 minutes. Cream the butter and the sugar together. Add the eggs and mix well. Stir in the oatmeal. In a separate bowl, whisk together the flour, baking soda, cinnamon, and salt. Add to the oatmeal mixture.

Spoon the batter into 2 greased and floured 9-inch cake pans. Bake for 25 to 30 minutes, or until a tester comes clean. Remove the cakes from the pans and let cool.

Meanwhile, prepare the frosting. Mix all of the frosting ingredients in a heavy pot and cook over medium heat for 5 minutes, stirring constantly. Remove from the heat and let cool slightly. Place a layer of frosting on one of the cakes. Place the other cake on top and frost the top as well.

Makes 8 to 10 servings

— THE DAVY JACKSON INN

Sweet Prune Cakes with Buttermilk Vanilla Sauce

Make these cakes in the mini-bundt pans and they appear to be a royal crown on the tea table. The inn serves this often, and guests are surprised to learn that prunes give the sweetest taste to these little jewels.

CAKES
1½ cups sugar
 ¾ cup vegetable oil
 3 eggs, beaten
 1 teaspoon vanilla extract
 1 cup buttermilk
 2 cups all-purpose flour
 1 teaspoon baking powder
 1 teaspoon baking soda
½ teaspoon salt
 1 teaspoon ground cinnamon
 1 teaspoon grated nutmeg
 1 teaspoon ground allspice
 1 cup pitted baby prunes, finely
   chopped

SAUCE
½ cup sugar
¼ cup buttermilk
½ cup (1 stick) butter
1 teaspoon vanilla extract

GARNISHES
Mint leaves
Raspberries

Preheat the oven to 300°. In a medium bowl, combine the sugar, oil, eggs, vanilla, and buttermilk. Mix well. In a large bowl, whisk together the flour, baking powder, baking soda, salt, and spices. Add the buttermilk mixture to the dry ingredients, stirring well. Fold in the prunes.

Pour the batter into 10 mini-bundt cups, about ¾ full. Bake for 35 to 40 minutes, or until cakes spring back when touched. Cool on a wire rack for about 45 minutes. Invert the pans onto a baking sheet. Wait 10 minutes before removing the bundt pans to release the cakes.

To prepare the sauce, combine all of the ingredients in a double boiler. Cook until warm and thoroughly combined. Pour over the cakes and serve. Garnish with mint and a raspberry.

Makes 10 cakes

— *THE DAVY JACKSON INN*

A Cowboy's Chocolate Chip Cookies

While we taped the show at the Inn at 410, we listened to the lyrical strains of a cowboy poet as we sipped cider and ate these incredible cookies. The inn serves these on special occasions and sometimes during check-in time. The grains, seeds, and granola make for a hearty sweet cookie that innkeeper Sally Krueger credits to the Babbling Brook Inn in Santa Cruz, California. She changed the original recipe by adding the raspberry creme granola and the sunflower seeds. This recipe makes a lot of cookies. You may freeze the dough and use as needed or make all of the cookies and freeze them.

2 cups all-purpose flour
1 teaspoon baking powder
1 teaspoon baking soda
¼ teaspoon salt
1 cup (2 sticks) margarine
1 cup packed brown sugar
1 cup sugar
2 eggs
1 teaspoon vanilla extract
1 cup white chocolate chips

1 cup semisweet chocolate chips
1½ cups raisins
1 cup chopped nuts
½ cup toasted sunflower seeds
1½ cups toasted old-fashioned oats
1½ cups granola, such as raspberry creme or your favorite kind

Preheat the oven to 375°. In a medium bowl, sift together the flour, baking powder, baking soda, and salt. Stir to combine. Set aside.

In a large bowl of electric mixer, cream together the margarine and the sugars. Add the eggs and vanilla and beat until well blended. Add the dry ingredients and beat well.

Transfer the cookie dough to a large bowl and stir in the chocolate chips, raisins, nuts, sunflower seeds, oats, and granola. When well mixed (Sally likes to say you need a cowboy-sized grip and lasso-twisting arm to mix this well), use a 1 1/2-inch or so cookie scoop and place balls on an ungreased cookie sheet and flatten slightly. Leave 1 1/2 inches or so of space between the cookies. Bake for 10 minutes, or until barely gold. Best when slightly undercooked.

Makes 8 dozen

— *THE INN AT 410*

Ragout of Lamb
with Garden Vegetables

A LIGHT AT THE INN

Appetizers, Entrées, Side Dishes, Desserts

Appetizers

Sweet-and-Spicy Shrimp Kebobs al Fresco

Although most often used as an appetizer, you may also serve this dish as an entrée with a mixed green salad. (See Chef Jon Emanuel's recipe for Dill-Dijon Salad Dressing on page 133 to go with the salad.) At the inn, they use Alaskan Spot Prawns but any fresh shrimp will do. You will need 12 bamboo skewers.

SHRIMP
36 medium to large raw shrimp, peeled, tail on, deveined

BASTING SAUCE:
⅓ cup butter, melted
¼ cup honey
2 tablespoons Thai paste (or substitute with red pepper flakes)

Juice of ½ lime
1 tablespoon chopped Cilantro
1 garlic clove, minced
1½ teaspoons grated fresh gingerroot
1 tablespoon sesame oil
Salt and white pepper to taste

Preheat a greased grill to high. Take 6 shrimp and run 2 skewers through them, one on either side of the shrimp, so that they will lie flat and even on the grill. Continue with all of the shrimp until they are skewered; set aside. Combine all of the basting ingredients. Place the shrimp on the grill and baste immediately. Close the grill cover for 1 minute. Open and baste again and flip the skewers over; baste again. Watch carefully, and as the shrimp are just about done (it should take only 2 to 3 minutes on a hot grill) close the cover for 30 seconds to glaze. Be careful not to overcook. Remove the shrimp from the grill and serve immediately.

Makes 6 appetizer servings

— GLACIER BAY COUNTRY INN

Red Pepper Polenta Tostada

Built like the mountains that surround this charming Victorian getaway, the tostada is exciting to look at and tastes delicious. Make small disks out of polenta and stack them with a filling of goat cheese and mushrooms. Each August, the town of Telluride hosts a wild mushroom festival in celebration of the harvest season in the mountain forests around this old mining town. This dish celebrates the mushroom bounty. The polenta needs to cool; you can make this dish several hours ahead or the day before.

POLENTA
1 cup chicken stock
1 cup half-and-half
1 roasted red pepper, peeled, seeded, and puréed
1 cup semolina flour
1 tablespoon shredded Parmesan cheese
½ teaspoon cayenne pepper
½ cup (1 stick) butter
Salt and pepper
Canola oil for sautéing

FILLING
2 cloves garlic
Olive, oil for coating and sauteing
5- to 6-ounce mix of Swiss chard, dandelion greens, spinach, and arugula
8 ounces shiitake mushrooms, crimini, morels, or other wild mushrooms in season
1 ounce goat cheese
1 ounce cream cheese
2 fresh chipotle peppers
1 cup sour cream

In a medium saucepan, combine the stock, the half-and-half, and the red pepper purée. When the mixture comes to a boil, whisk in the semolina. Stir and cook over low heat until thickened and beginning to pull away from the sides of the pan, about 20 minutes. Add the Parmesan, cayenne, and butter. Stir until combined. Season to taste. Let cool completely.

Once cooled, spoon about 2 tablespoons polenta between 2 sheets of plastic wrap. Flatten and shape with the palm of your hand into a round disk, about ⅛-inch thick. Remove the disk and place on wax paper. Repeat with remaining polenta to make 8 to 10 tostadas. Refrigerate if not ready to use.

Preheat the oven to 350°. Lightly coat garlic cloves with a little olive oil and set in a small ovenproof pan. Place in the oven and roast until brown, about 15 minutes. Remove from the oven. Peel and mash the cloves. Heat 2 tablespoons olive oil in a large sauté pan until the heat moves the oil in the pan. Sear the greens along with the garlic until limp but not lifeless. Put them on a plate and let cool. While the oven is still on, toss the mushrooms with a little olive oil and a seasoning of salt and pepper. Lay the mushrooms on a baking sheet and roast for 5 to 7 minutes.

Using a fork, combine the 2 cheeses in a small bowl and set aside.

In a blender, purée the chipotle peppers with the sour cream, just until blended.

Heat 1 tablespoon of canola oil in a medium sauté pan. Place the chilled tostadas in the pan and sauté until stiff. Turn.

To assemble the dish, first spoon the chipotle and sour cream mixture onto each plate; place a tostada in the center of each serving plate. Evenly divide the greens and the mushrooms. Layer with a second tostada. Cover with the cheese mixture and serve.

Makes 4 servings

— *SAN SOPHIA INN*

Tortilla Pinwheels

Roll up tortillas filled with chilies and cheese and serve with salsa, and you have an easy hors d'oeuvre that goes fast. You may want to make a double batch of these if serving more than four guests.

6 ounces cream cheese, softened
2 ounces sour cream
1 can (4 ounces) chopped black olives
¼ cup chopped green chilies
2 large flour tortillas

Combine the cream cheese and sour cream. Fold in the olives and green chilies. Spread right to the edge of each tortilla. Roll up and slice to about ¾-inch thickness. Serve with salsa.

Makes 16 bite-size pinwheels

— *APACHE CANYON RANCH*

69

Fiddlehead-and-Lobster Soufflé

Blue Hill Inn Chef André Strong has a knack for making some of the best soufflés outside of France. The inn's menu is chockablock with soufflés for appetizers, entrées, and desserts. This one incorporates two Maine ingredients—fiddlehead ferns (so named because they look like the head of a fiddle; they taste something like asparagus) that grow wild throughout New England, and lobster, trapped only a short distance away. Chef Strong says the secret to the success of a good soufflé is to work with really fresh eggs. You will need to begin the recipe at least 2 hours ahead of serving time.

4 tablespoons coarse sea salt
2½ pounds live lobsters, or 1 pound fresh lobster meat
1 pound trimmed fiddleheads (brown leaves and tough ends discarded), or asparagus tips
2 cups whole milk
½ teaspoon ground black pepper
1 teaspoon fine sea salt
3 tablespoons melted unsalted butter
5 large eggs, separated
5 additional large egg whites
Butter and flour for coating

Bring 3 quarts of water to a boil in a large covered stockpot and add 3 tablespoons of the coarse salt. Place the lobsters into the boiling water, and as soon as the water returns to a boil, cook the lobsters for 5 minutes. Drain and rinse them. This should yield about 1 pound meat. (Skip this step if using already prepared lobster.) Pick out the meat and cut it into ½-inch dice. Refrigerate in a covered bowl over ice.

Bring 6 quarts of water to a boil in a large stockpot with the remaining 1 tablespoon sea salt. Add the fiddleheads, cover the pot, and boil for about 8 minutes. Drain and rinse under cold water. Purée the fiddleheads in a food processor with a steel blade for 2 minutes, pausing a couple of times to scrape the sides down with a spatula. Keep the processor running and gradually add the milk. Process for another 2 minutes or until smooth. Transfer the mixture to a heavy-bottomed 6-quart saucepan over very low heat. Add the ground pepper, fine sea salt, and the melted butter. Whisk in the egg yolks, one at a time, until thoroughly combined. Continue to whisk occasionally until the mixture thickens slightly and starts to steam; do not let mixture simmer or boil. This will take about 15 to 30 minutes, depending on how low your heat really is. Let mixture cool to room temperature; keep in refrigerator if sitting out for more than 1 hour.

One hour before serving time, preheat the oven to 425°. Butter and flour eight 8-ounce soufflé dishes or ramekins; set aside.

About ½ hour before serving, rub a clean, dry, large stainless-steel bowl with half of a lemon. Add 10 egg whites and beat with a high-speed mixer until stiff but not dry. Into another large stainless steel bowl, spoon the fiddlehead mixture and fold in about ⅓ of the egg-whites. Add the remaining egg whites and fold until incorporated, but not beaten down. Fill each ramekin half-full with the mixture. Add lobster pieces to each and fill with remaining soufflé mixture. Place ramekins in the oven. Cook 20 minutes, or until soufflés are fluffy and risen and partially brown on top. Remove with large tongs and serve immediately.

Makes 8 servings

— *BLUE HILL INN*

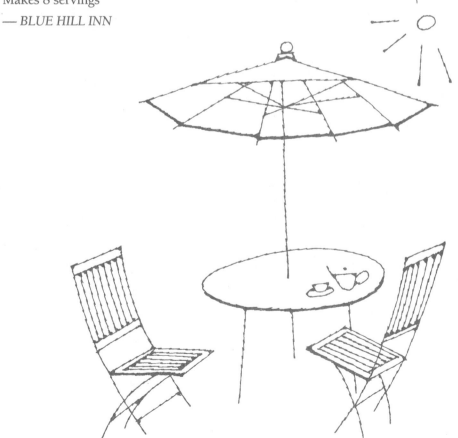

Crawfish in Spicy Creole Sauce

Crawfish, or crayfish, resemble tiny lobsters. They are sweet and may be cooked as you do most crustaceans. Boil them just until they turn pink or bright red.

¼ cup creole or hot mustard
½ cup olive oil
¼ cup rice-wine vinegar
1 tablespoon fresh lime juice
2 tablespoons Worcestershire
   sauce
1 teaspoon minced garlic
1 tablespoon ketchup
½ teaspoon Tabasco
½ teaspoon paprika
   Grated rind of ½ lemon

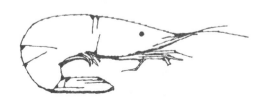

1 tablespoon chopped fresh
   parsley
1 tablespoon finely chopped
   green onion
   Ground black pepper
   Lettuce
1 pound crawfish tails, cooked
¾ cup celery root, cut into
   julienne
1 roasted red bell pepper, cut
   into julienne

In a medium-sized mixing bowl, combine all of the ingredients except the lettuce, the crawfish, celery root, and roasted pepper. Cover and refrigerate until ready to serve.

When ready to serve, line each individual serving plate with a bed of lettuce. Evenly divide the crawfish, piling them in the center of the lettuce bed. Garnish with the celery root and roasted peppers. Place a dollop of the dipping sauce on the side of the seafood or in a small bowl.

Makes 4 to 6 servings

— *INN AT LE ROSIER*

Wild Mushroom and Gruyère Potato Latkes

At the Notchland Inn, creative Chef Laurel Tessier serves these potato pan-cakes as an appetizer, but they would also make a nice lunch dish.

3 Yukon Gold potatoes, unpeeled and cubed
1 tablespoon butter
1 medium onion, finely chopped
6 ounces wild mushroom assortment (such as shiitake, king, oyster, criminis), coarsely chopped
½ cup port wine
1 egg
2 sprigs fresh dill, finely chopped

2 tablespoons fresh, unseasoned bread crumbs
Kosher salt
Ground black pepper
4 ounces Gruyère cheese, shredded
1 cup vegetable oil
4 ounces Prosciutto, thinly sliced and cut into ½-inch width strips by 3 inches long

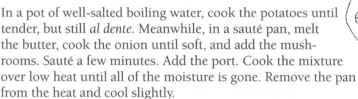

In a pot of well-salted boiling water, cook the potatoes until tender, but still *al dente*. Meanwhile, in a sauté pan, melt the butter, cook the onion until soft, and add the mushrooms. Sauté a few minutes. Add the port. Cook the mixture over low heat until all of the moisture is gone. Remove the pan from the heat and cool slightly.

Place the potatoes in a large bowl and mash slightly with a large spoon. Add the mushroom mixture, the egg, the dill, the 2 tablespoons of the bread crumbs, and season with salt and pepper. Mix and then stir in half of the cheese.

Heat the oil in a large skillet. Shape the potato mixture into 3-inch patties and coat with the remaining cheese and a few strands of the prosciutto.

Makes 4 to 6 servings

— *THE NOTCHLAND INN*

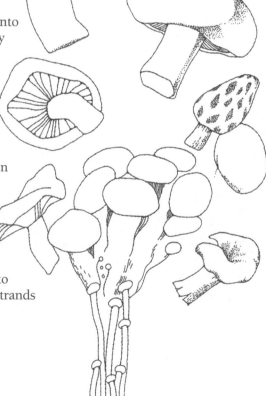

Baked Trout Phyllo Bundles with Watercress Sauce

Watercress and trout naturally go together. In the wild they are both found in clean, cold, moving water. At the inn, they serve a combination of fresh and smoked trout wrapped in delicate phyllo dough and topped with a watercress cream sauce, using cress found right by the stream that runs along the inn's property.

SAUCE
- ¼ cup finely chopped shallots
- 2 tablespoons butter
- 1 large bunch watercress (2 cups or more), washed and tough stems removed
- ¾ cup whipping cream
- Salt and pepper

CRUMB MIX
- 1½ slices day-old bread (the inn uses potato bread)
- 2 teaspoons minced garlic
- 2 teaspoons minced shallots
- Meat of ½ smoked trout (discard any skin and bones)

STUFFING
- 2 small rainbow trout filets
- 1 tablespoon butter
- ½ lemon
- ⅛ teaspoon hot sauce, or to taste

BUNDLES
- 4 sheets phyllo dough, cut into quarters
- ¼ cup (½ stick) butter, melted

GARNISH
- Lemon wedges
- Watercress sprigs

To prepare the sauce, sauté the shallots in 2 tablespoons butter over medium heat until they begin to soften. Add the watercress and stir until it wilts but is still bright green. Add the cream. Increase the heat to high and bring to a boil. Remove from the heat. Purée the sauce in a blender until smooth. Transfer to a small saucepan. Season with salt and pepper to taste. Keep warm.

Prepare the crumb mixture by chopping the bread into coarse crumbs in a food processor. Add the minced garlic, shallots, and smoked trout and process again until the trout is finely and evenly mixed. Set aside.

To prepare fresh trout, sauté the filets, skin side down, in the butter in a small skillet over medium heat for a minute or so, only until the edges of the fish begin to turn opaque. Turn the fish out onto a paper towel, skin-side up. Peel off the skin and discard. Squeeze the lemon onto the fish; adding several drops of hot sauce. Brush to coat evenly. Cut each filet into 4 pieces.

Preheat the oven to 375° and prepare the bundles by laying out 2

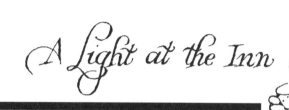

phyllo quarters. Brush 1 with melted butter and place the other sheet on top. Place 1 tablespoon of the crumb mixture at 1 end of the rectangle, about 2 inches from the end. Place a piece of fish on top of the crumbs. Gently wrap the fish in the pastry, first folding up the 2-inch end and then folding in each side.

Sprinkle more bread crumbs on the unrolled portion of the phyllo and continue to fold the bundle over until the pastry completely surrounds the fish. Brush the top of the bundle with more melted butter. Bake on ungreased sheet pans for about 10 minutes, or until the crust is golden brown. To serve, whisk the sauce over the heat. Place 2 phyllo bundles on each plate and top with watercress sauce. Garnish with lemon wedges and watercress.

Makes 4 servings

— *INN AT VAUCLUSE SPRING*

Seared Tuna and Snapper with Wild Fennel

Chef Gerard Reversade finds wild fennel growing not too far from the inn. It is his secret hiding place. You and I just have to substitute with sprigs of fresh fennel from our grocery or come out to Maui, and I think Gerard can be coaxed into telling all where he hunts down his fennel.

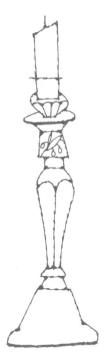

2 tablespoons peanut oil
4 ounces fresh tuna steak, cut into ¼-inch slices
4 ounces red snapper filets, cut into ¼-inch slices
Salt and pepper
2 tablespoons lemon juice
½ cup olive oil
2 tablespoons finely chopped green onion

2 seedless Hawaiian peppers or chili peppers, finely diced
4 teaspoons finely chopped fresh ginger
4 whole Chinese parsley leaves (or substitute with curly-leaf parsley)
4 or more sprigs wild fennel
1 Japanese or English cucumber, peeled and finely sliced

In a hot skillet, heat the peanut oil and sear the tuna and the snapper until they are just pink inside. Season with salt and pepper. Place the fish in a decorative pattern on a platter. Pour the lemon juice over the fish, followed by the oil, green onion, pepper, and ginger. Artfully arrange the Chinese parsley, wild fennel, and the cucumber on the plate.

Makes 4 servings

— *THE PLANTATION INN/GERARD'S RESTAURANT*

Broiled Chesapeake Oysters with Roasted Pepper Salsa

Chef Scott Daniels developed this signature recipe for the inn and its Krazy Kats Restaurant. The oysters are baked and then topped with a sweet-and-tangy fresh salsa. The oysters are then broiled with a lemon-cheese sauce crust or gratinée. Begin the recipe by having a pot of simmering water on the stove.

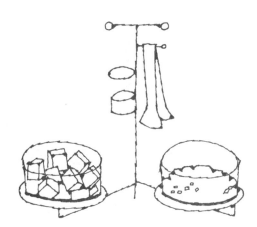

OYSTERS
- 2 dozen large oysters
- 4 egg yolks
- ¼ cup white wine
- 10 ounces clarified butter
- Juice and grated rind of 1 lemon
- Tabasco to taste
- ¼ cup Parmesan cheese
- Ground black pepper to taste

SALSA
- 2 red bell peppers, roasted, peeled, and cut julienne
- 2 yellow bell peppers, roasted, peeled, and cut julienne
- 2 green bell peppers, roasted, peeled, and cut julienne
- 3 shallots, minced
- ¼ cup packed minced fresh cilantro
- ½ cup olive oil
- ¼ cup lime juice
- Salt and pepper to taste

Place the egg yolks in a stainless-steel bowl; add the white wine and whisk until incorporated. Place the bowl over the simmering water. Whisk the eggs steadily till medium-stiff peaks form. Remove from the heat and gradually add the clarified butter while whisking. Add the lemon juice and rind and the Tabasco. Fold the cheese and black pepper into the mixture. Keep warm until ready to assemble.

Shuck the oysters, discarding the top half of the shells. Just loosen the meat from the bottom half of the shells and place them in the refrigerator until ready to use.

Meanwhile, prepare the salsa. Combine the peppers with the remaining ingredients; set aside.

Preheat the oven to 400°. Place the oysters on a layer of rock salt in a baking pan and bake for 5 minutes. Remove from the oven and turn on the broiler. Place 1 tablespoon of the salsa on each oyster, then 1 tablespoon of the cheese mixture. Place under the broiler and broil just until the tops turn golden.

Makes 4 servings

— *THE INN AT MONTCHANIN VILLAGE*

Entrées

PASTA

Homemade Orecchiette Pasta with Broccoli

My mother used to make something like this dish when we were growing up. Today, with the availability of fine olive oils, fresh pasta, and imported cheeses, it has taken on a different flavor at my house. If you do not have time to make the fresh orecchiette, dried is available. The combination of anchovy flavor, vinegar, spices, and water is the heart of the flavor presented in this Tuscan-style dish.

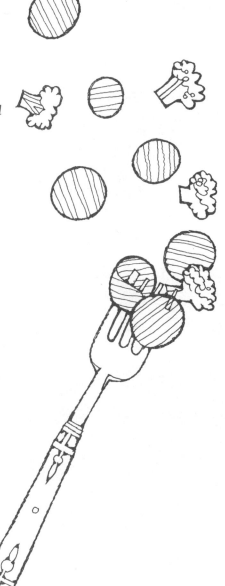

1 pound broccoli florets, cut into 1-inch pieces
3 tablespoons minced fresh garlic
3 tablespoons anchovy paste
4 tablespoons olive oil

1 pound fresh orecchiette pasta (Homemade Pasta on page 138)
Freshly ground pepper
½ cup finely grated Parmigiana-Reggiano cheese

Bring 5 quarts of water to a boil and cook the broccoli florets for about 3 minutes, or until *al dente*. While the broccoli cooks, heat the olive oil in a large sauté pan or Dutch oven and sauté the garlic with the anchovy paste for 3 to 4 minutes.

Remove the broccoli from the water with a slotted spoon. Add the pasta, keeping the water at a full boil. Cook the pasta until *al dente*, for about 1 minute; drain, reserving 1 cup of pasta water.

Add the reserved pasta water to the garlic and anchovy sauté pan. Add the pasta and broccoli to the mixture. Add pepper to taste. Heat through and serve immediately with the grated cheese.

Makes 4 to 6 servings

— *THE CAPTAIN FREEMAN INN*

Crabmeat Ravioli with Fresh Tomato Burgundy Sauce

Note: Both the sauce (2 hours) and the ravioli filling (4 hours) must be prepared ahead of time. Do the filling first.

SAUCE

- ½ cup extra-virgin olive oil
- 4 cloves garlic, minced
- 1 cup diced onion
- 10 pounds Roma tomatoes, halved
- 1 cup Burgundy wine
- ¼ cup sugar
- 2 tablespoons chopped fresh basil
- 1 tablespoon salt
- 1 tablespoon freshly ground black pepper

RAVIOLI

- ¾ pound fresh jumbo lump crabmeat, cleaned
- 1½ ounces mozzarella cheese, shredded
- ½ pound ricotta cheese
- 2 tablespoons snipped fresh chives
- 2 tablespoons minced scallions
- ¼ cup bread crumbs
- 1 egg
- 10 fresh pasta sheets, 10 x 12 inches

Prepare the sauce. Pour the olive oil, garlic, and onions into a 3-gallon stockpot over medium heat. Cook, stirring constantly, until the garlic and onions are tender. Add the tomatoes, wine, sugar, basil, salt, and pepper. Simmer over low heat for 2 hours, stirring every 15 to 20 minutes. Keep the sauce warm until ready to serve.

For the ravioli filling, combine the crabmeat, mozzarella, ricotta, chives, scallions, bread crumbs, and egg in a large bowl. Mix well using a rubber spatula. Refrigerate for at least 3 hours.

Arrange 2 of the pasta sheets on a lightly floured surface and cut each sheet into 6 square pieces. Brush the outer edges of all the pasta squares with a little water. Spoon about 1½ tablespoons of the chilled crab mixture into the center of half of the pasta squares. Gently place the remaining pasta squares over the filled ones, pressing the edges to seal. Repeat with the remaining pasta sheets and filling. Chill for 1 hour.

Cook the ravioli in a large pot of salted, boiling water for 5 minutes. Top with the sauce and serve immediately.

Makes 4 to 6 servings

— *INN AT OLDE NEW BERLIN*

Homemade Linguine with Clam Sauce

This traditional pasta recipe will turn even those who are not clam lovers into clam diggers. The hint of tomato in the sauce laces the recipe with delicate tastes of Italy. Carol Edmondson, the innkeeper/chef, catches fresh clams on the beach just down the street from the inn. How romantic, in spite of the abundance of garlic!

6 dozen littleneck or 24 qua-
  hogs or chowder clams
½ cup cornmeal
4 large cloves garlic, minced
2 cups fresh vine-ripened tomatoes, cut into ½-inch pieces, or
  canned diced tomatoes with
  their juice

3 tablespoons olive oil
½ cup finely chopped fresh basil
  Freshly ground pepper and
  salt

Wash the clams thoroughly under running water and soak them for several hours or overnight in a sink full of water with ½ cup cornmeal sprinkled over the top. The clams will ingest the cornmeal, which causes them to expel any sand still in their systems.

About 45 minutes before serving time, rinse the soaked clams under cold running water. Place the clams in a large Dutch oven with 4 cups of fresh water. Bring the water to a boil over high heat, then cover and turn off the heat. About 10 minutes later, remove the clams from the pot, reserving the water in the Dutch oven. Save only the clams whose shells have partially opened; discard any that have remained closed. Remove the clams from their shells; chop the meat coarsely into small pieces, reserving any liquid. Set aside.

Sauté the garlic and tomatoes in the olive oil for 3 to 4 minutes. Meanwhile, cook the linguine in the boiling water for 1 minute or until *al dente* and drain. Add the linguine to the garlic and tomatoes, followed by 1 cup of the reserved clam liquid, the chopped clams, and the basil. Cook for 1 minute, or just long enough to combine flavors. Season with salt and pepper. Serve at once.

Makes 4 to 6 servings

— *THE CAPTAIN FREEMAN INN*

Seafood

North Carolina Seafood Gumbo

Chef Elmo Barnes is absolutely passionate about the food he cooks. Totally trained by his mother and grandmother, he devises his own home-made combinations with the only prerequisite that they be full of flavor. This gumbo has it all, and Elmo calls it the finest gumbo ever. Like many southern one-pot meal recipes, a roux is the basis for the recipe. Here, it is one made with vegetables and mushrooms. You only need one cup as the recipe states, so save any left over for another recipe. If you would like a homemade Cajun sauce, Elmo bottles his own at the inn. Call him there (see Inn Directory to order some).

ROUX

- 1 tablespoon olive oil
- 2 pounds onions, coarsely chopped
- 6 spring onions with tops, finely sliced
- 1 pound mushrooms, sliced
- 6 to 8 garlic cloves, thinly sliced
- 1 red bell pepper, cut into ½-inch dice
- 2 tablespoons meat grease or bacon fat
- 2 tablespoons shortening
- 2 tablespoons olive oil
- ½ teaspoon salt
- 1 teaspoon Cajun spice
- 1 cup all-purpose flour Cold water for thinning
- ¼ cup soy sauce
- ¼ cup steak sauce

GUMBO

- 1 pound kielbasa sausage
- 1 pound skinless, boneless chicken parts
- ¼ pound medium shrimp, cleaned
- ¼ pound flounder filets, cut into bite-size pieces
- ¼ pound bay scallops
- ¾ pound small clams
- 1 pound beef stew meat, cut into bite-size pieces
- 4 cans (each 14½ ounces) chicken broth
- 3 large onions, coarsely diced
- 1 cup coarsely diced celery
- 1 cup coarsely diced carrots
- 1½ cups fresh corn kernels, or substitute with 12 ounces canned corn niblets
- 1 can (12 ounces) tomatoes with juice
- 2 cups sliced fresh okra, or 2 packages (each 10 ounces) frozen
- ¼ cup olive oil
- 1 cup homemade roux

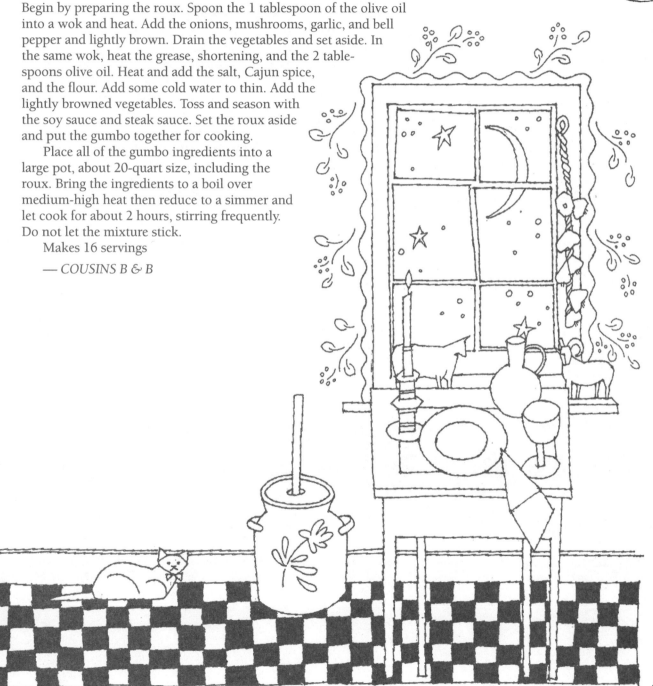

Begin by preparing the roux. Spoon the 1 tablespoon of the olive oil into a wok and heat. Add the onions, mushrooms, garlic, and bell pepper and lightly brown. Drain the vegetables and set aside. In the same wok, heat the grease, shortening, and the 2 table-spoons olive oil. Heat and add the salt, Cajun spice, and the flour. Add some cold water to thin. Add the lightly browned vegetables. Toss and season with the soy sauce and steak sauce. Set the roux aside and put the gumbo together for cooking.

Place all of the gumbo ingredients into a large pot, about 20-quart size, including the roux. Bring the ingredients to a boil over medium-high heat then reduce to a simmer and let cook for about 2 hours, stirring frequently. Do not let the mixture stick.

Makes 16 servings

— *COUSINS B & B*

Barbecued-Marinated Trout with Onion-Caper Relish

The inn is located in trout-fishing territory, and I found trout barbecued this way to be bursting with flavor. Add this splendid and colorful relish and you will find this a winning recipe with your own guests and family. The relish may be prepared up to 2 days in advance. Cover well and refrigerate. Rewarm when ready to serve with the trout. The trout needs to marinate for 2 hours before cooking. This recipe hails from the inn's creative and unusual cookbook, Thyme & the River Too, *available from the inn.*

MARINADE
- 4 trout filets, each 8 ounces
- ½ cup olive oil
- ¼ cup lemon juice
- 1 tablespoon minced onion
- 1 clove garlic, minced
- ¼ teaspoon salt
- ¼ teaspoon black pepper
- 1 teaspoon dillweed
- 1 teaspoon sugar

RELISH
- 1 tablespoon olive oil
- ½ cup finely chopped yellow onion
- ½ cup finely chopped red onion
- ½ cup finely chopped red bell pepper
- 1 clove garlic, minced
- ½ teaspoon finely minced lemon rind
- 1 tablespoon drained small capers
- 1 tablespoon tomato paste
- 2 tablespoons minced fresh flat-leaf parsley
- Salt and pepper

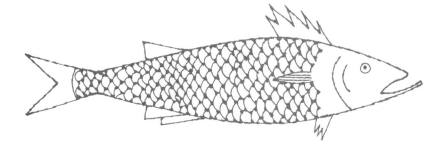

Place the trout in a nonreactive baking dish. Whisk together the olive oil, lemon juice, onion, garlic, salt, pepper, dill, and sugar. Pour over the trout and marinate in the refrigerator for 2 hours.

To make the relish, heat the olive oil in a medium-sized skillet. Add the onions, red pepper, and garlic. Sauté over medium-high heat for about 5 minutes, stirring constantly. Add the lemon rind, capers, tomato paste, and parsley, mixing well. Cook for another 2 minutes. Season with salt and pepper to taste. Serve on the side of the trout.

Prepare the barbecue grill. When ready, place the trout, skin side down, on aluminum foil on the grill. Barbecue for 8 to 10 minutes, until the meat flakes easily with a fork. Remove from the grill and garnish with the relish.

Makes 6 to 8 servings

— *THE STEAMBOAT INN*

Chesapeake Crab Cakes

Crab cakes are a tradition, particularly along the Eastern Shore of Maryland. The William Page Inn is primarily a bed-and-breakfast, but every now and then a little crab cake makes its way onto the breakfast tray or as an evening snack.

3 slices white bread, torn into bite-size pieces

2 teaspoons water
1 pound fresh lump crabmeat, drained, flaked, and picked clean
2 eggs, beaten
1½ tablespoons mayonnaise
1½ tablespoons Worcestershire sauce
1½ tablespoons chopped fresh parsley
1½ teaspoons stone-ground mustard
1½ teaspoons Old Bay seasoning
¼ teaspoon salt
¼ cup (½ stick) butter

Place the bread in a large bowl. Sprinkle with the water, just to moisten. Add the crabmeat, eggs, mayonnaise, Worcestershire sauce, parsley, mustard, Old Bay seasonings, and salt. Mix together; mixture should be lumpy. Shape into 6 patties. Melt the butter in a sauté pan and cook each crab cake on both sides until golden brown. Alternately you may bake the crab cakes on a lightly greased baking sheet in a 500° oven for 12 minutes, or until golden brown.

Makes 6 servings

— *THE WILLIAM PAGE INN*

Sautéed Halibut with Olive-Chili Relish

Well, here it is—the Glacier Bay Country Inn's most requested recipe as Chef Jon Emanuel explains: "The halibut is topped with an olive-based relish called muffaletta. *Muffaletta is great with many things and is an all-around condiment for sandwiches and party dips or in pasta salads. The relish is colorful and bursting with flavor."*

RELISH
- 1 cup green pimento-stuffed olives
- ¾ cup black or Kalamata olives, pitted
- ½ cup roasted, peeled, seeded Anaheim chilies or 1 can (4 ounce) mild green chilies, finely chopped
- ½ ounce anchovy filet
- 2 teaspoons capers
- ¼ cup whole- or coarse-grain mustard
- 1½ teaspoons dried oregano
- 1 tablespoon chopped fresh parsley
- 1 tablespoon chopped fresh basil
- 2 tablespoons extra-virgin olive oil
  Juice of 1 lemon

HALIBUT
- 6 halibut filets, each 6 ounces
- ½ cup bread flour
- 3 tablespoons salt
- 1 tablespoon pepper
- 4 ounces olive oil
  Juice of ½ lemon

Place all of the ingredients for the relish into a food processor. Chop to a coarse consistency. Let the relish sit in the refrigerator for 1 hour before using.

To prepare the halibut, combine the flour, salt, and pepper. Heat the oil in a large skillet over medium-high heat. Dip the filets into the flour; shake off the excess, and add to the skillet. Sauté the filets, turning once, until cooked to medium, about 3 to 4 minutes per side. Drizzle with lemon juice; remove from the pan, and drain. Place on heated plates and top with the relish.

Makes 6 servings

— *GLACIER BAY COUNTRY INN*

Wolf-fish in Potato Crust with Chervil Sauce

Chef André Strong created a one-dish meal here. The fish is baked between fanned layers of scalloped potatoes. Wolf-fish is a firm-fleshed fish that can be substituted with salmon or striped bass; just make sure to adjust the cooking time according to thickness.

2 tablespoons sea salt
3 pounds Yukon Gold potatoes, peeled
3 ounces clarified butter (from 5 ounces unsalted butter)
1 teaspoon salt
½ teaspoon ground black pepper
2 tablespoons coarsely chopped fresh chervil

3 pounds skinless, boneless wolf-fish filets, cut into 6-ounce pieces

SAUCE
2½ cups heavy cream
2 tablespoons water
2 cups lightly packed chervil, stems removed, chopped
Salt and pepper

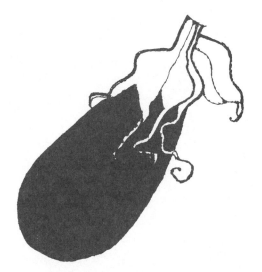

Butter a baking pan 12 x 18 inches. Bring a stockpot of water to a boil and add the sea salt.

Slice the potatoes into very thin rounds, about ¹⁄₁₆ inch. Add the rounds to the boiling water and cook for 1 minute. Drain and transfer to a large mixing bowl.

Preheat the oven to 425°. Add the clarified butter, salt, pepper, and the 2 tablespoons of the chervil to the potatoes. Mix thoroughly with your fingers, taking care not to break the potato rounds. Dealing like playing cards, carefully cover the bottom of the buttered baking pan with the potato rounds, overlapping as you go. Place the fish pieces equidistant in the pan. Cover each piece of fish with overlapping potato rounds until all of the potatoes are in the pan and the fish is fully crusted.

Bake in the oven for 30 to 40 minutes, just until the fish is opaque. Brown the potato crust under the broiler before serving.

While the fish bakes, place the cream in a heavy 2-quart pan; cook over moderately high heat to reduce the cream to about 1 cup, stirring often; do not burn. Add the water and the chervil to the cream and simmer for 5 to 10 minutes. Season with salt and pepper and serve with the fish.

Makes 8 servings

— BLUE HILL INN

Monkfish Medallions with Spinach, Leeks, and Curry

The flavor of monkfish has been compared to that of lobster. In recent years, monkfish has become a sought-after delicacy, and with the abundance of fresh seafood in Maine, this is almost always on the menu. Chef André Strong suggests serving it with saffron-laced basmati rice.

3 pounds monkfish filets, skin and membranes removed

2 tablespoons clarified butter (from 4 tablespoons unsalted butter)

½ cup all-purpose flour

1 tablespoon curry powder

1 teaspoon fine sea salt

3 tablespoons plus ½ pound (2 sticks) unsalted butter Salt and pepper

1½ pounds leeks, white and green parts, weighed after they are trimmed and cleaned

3 ounces shallots, chopped medium fine

1 cup dry white wine

3 tablespoons Champagne vinegar

2 teaspoons medium-hot curry powder

1 tablespoon clarified butter

2 cups basmati or other rice seasoned with saffron and cooked

2 pounds fresh spinach, stems removed

3 tablespoons finely chopped cilantro

Cut the fish into 12 medallions, each 1-inch thick, and spread out on a baking sheet. Mix together the flour, curry powder, and salt, and dust the fish lightly through a sieve; turn fish over and repeat.

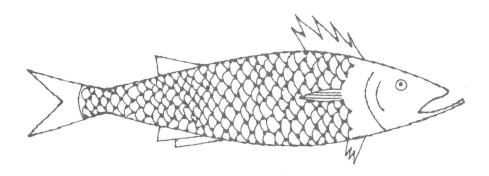

Steam the spinach in a covered steamer for 1 minute. After the water boils, turn off the heat. Add 1 tablespoon of the butter and salt and pepper to taste. Place the lid back on the pot.

Cut the leeks into 3-inch pieces and julienne each piece. Sauté them in 1 tablespoon of the butter until they are wilted. Add ¾ cup water and simmer, stirring occasionally, until the liquid has been absorbed, about 15 minutes.

Cut the ½ pound of butter into 16 even pieces and refrigerate. In a medium-sized nonreactive saucepan, sauté the chopped shallots in an additional tablespoon of butter over medium heat until translucent but not golden. Add the wine and vinegar. Reduce until one tablespoon of liquid remains. Lower the heat and whisk in the pieces of butter, a piece at a time. After 3 to 4 pieces, place back on the stove over lowest heat. Whisk in the rest of the butter, a piece at a time. Add curry powder and strain sauce into a small saucepan. Add salt and pepper to taste; keep warm on the lowest setting over a double boiler.

In a large nonstick frying pan, heat the clarified butter over high heat. Add the monkfish. Do not crowd the pan. Cook for 2 minutes on each side or just until cooked through and golden.

To assemble, place a bed of rice in the center of each plate. Flatten out to a circle. Cover the rice with a layer of spinach leaves, then a layer of leeks. Arrange 6 pieces of fish as the top layer; top with 2 tablespoons sauce; sprinkle with cilantro.

Makes 8 servings

— *BLUE HILL INN*

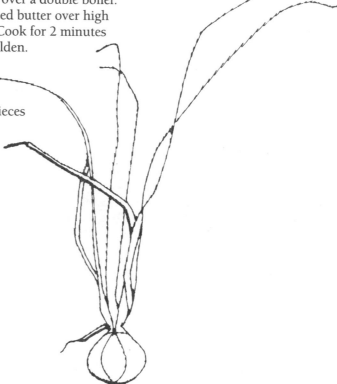

Roasted Grouper with Smoked Tomato Butter Sauce

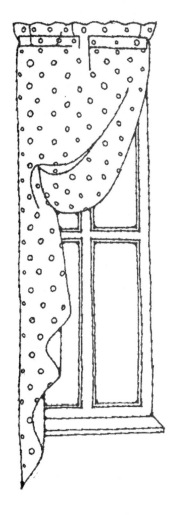

Grouper is suitable for frying, poaching, baking, or broiling, but always remove the tough outer skin before cooking.

2 cups dry white wine
2 tablespoons Champagne or rice-wine vinegar
1 tablespoon fresh lemon juice
½ cup smoked stewed tomatoes (may use canned), or use regular stewed tomatoes and add ⅛ teaspoon liquid smoke
½ cup sliced yellow onion
4 garlic bulbs, peeled and sliced into halves
2 tablespoons minced fresh parsley
1½ ounces heavy whipping cream

¼ cup Bloody Mary mix or tomato juice
½ pound (2 sticks) unsalted butter, chopped
2 teaspoons minced garlic
  Salt and white pepper
  Tabasco
½ teaspoon ground coriander
¼ teaspoon cayenne pepper
6 grouper filets, or any mild white fish, each 6 ounces
  Olive oil

Prepare the sauce first by combining the wine, vinegar, lemon juice, tomatoes, onion, garlic, and parsley in a medium saucepan. Bring to a boil over medium-high heat and cook until the sauce is completely reduced. Add the heavy whipping cream and Bloody Mary mix and cook until reduced by half. Lower the heat and gradually whisk in the unsalted butter. Add the garlic, salt, pepper, Tabasco to taste, coriander, and cayenne pepper. Check seasonings and adjust to taste. Strain the sauce and reserve it in a container submerged in hot, not boiling, water to keep warm.

Season the fish with salt. Heat a nonstick sauté pan to just smoking. Add olive oil to reach a depth of just under ¼ inch. Add the grouper, flesh side down, and cook, turning once, for 3 minutes on each side, or until golden brown. Remove the fish from the pan. Drain on paper towels and keep warm.

To serve, place 1 grouper filet, flesh side up, on each of 6 warm serving plates. Spoon the tomato sauce on and around each filet. Serve immediately.

Makes 6 servings

— *INN AT LE ROSIER*

Fire-Roasted Salmon with Molasses–Apple Cider Glaze

During the summer months Chef Sam Chapman bows to the tradition of those who settled the Pacific Northwest, and he makes a potlatch feast. The Indian word potlatch *means a gift. Years ago, it was a large dinner that a chief or warrior would give to his own and neighboring tribes. In the spirit of that tradition, Sam cooks the salmon outdoors on wood planks over a charcoal pit. Cooking the salmon in this manner, lightly chars the outside of the fish but keeps the inside tender and moist. Serve the salmon with another traditional Indian dish that Sam prepares,* Red Bean Succotash *(page 114). It is also delicious with mixed summer greens tossed in a vinaigrette dressing. You do not have to prepare as large a portion of salmon. At the end of this recipe, Sam also gives directions for cooking the salmon in the oven.*

Alderwood plank with sides long enough to hold the salmon (½ pound)
Olive oil
6 skinless salmon filets
Molasses-Apple Cider Glaze (page 133)

10-inch bamboo skewers
1 prepared barbecue firepit, coals red and glowing but without flames

Brush the alder plank with oil. Lay out the salmon and brush both sides with the Molasses–Apple Cider Glaze (page 133). Using bamboo skewers, secure the salmon to the plank in a crisscross fashion. Place the salmon over the coals and cook evenly until the fish is warmed through. You may finish the fish in a 400° oven.

Remove the salmon from the fire. Remove the skewers and cut the salmon into 4- to 6-ounce servings. Serve with Red Bean Succotash.

To prepare the fish entirely in the oven, preheat the oven to 425°. Cut hickory, cherry, cedar, or alderwood planks. Brush both sides of the fish with the glaze. Lightly oil the planks and place the fish on them. Bake for about 12 to 15 minutes, or until the salmon is cooked all the way through but is not dry.

Makes 6 servings

— *THE CAPTAIN WHIDBEY INN*

Shark with Fig Gravy

Chef Elmo Barnes won kudos for this dish at the annual Strange and Unusual Seafood Festival *in his town in 1994. Shark is caught off Beaufort, South Carolina, waters. When available, Elmo purchases shark off the docks. Halibut will also do here or other dense white fish. The fig gravy is delicious not only over fish but with other recipes, over mashed potatoes, for example.*

GRAVY
1 tablespoon olive oil
1 teaspoon butter
2 teaspoons minced garlic
⅓ cup all-purpose flour
1 can (14½ ounces) beef consommé or broth
½ cup finely chopped onion
½ cup small-dice green bell pepper
½ teaspoon salt
½ pint fig preserves
1 teaspoon paprika
½ teaspoon Cajun spice
8 ounces fatfree sour cream

SHARK
2 pounds shark or halibut filets
Salt and pepper
Steak sauce
Lemon-and-herb spice blend
1 tablespoon olive oil
1 tablespoon butter

Place the olive oil, butter, and 1 teaspoon of the garlic into a pre-heated wok. Add the flour and brown until it is a dark golden brown. Add the beef consommé and stir; be careful not to burn the gravy. If gravy is too thick, you may add a little water at any time. Add the onion and pepper and season with the salt. Simmer over medium heat until the vegetables are tender. Using a whisk, add the fig preserves, the remaining teaspoon of garlic, the paprika, and the Cajun spice. Fold in the sour cream. Cover and simmer over low heat for 10 minutes, stirring frequently. Set aside and prepare the shark.

Sprinkle each of the filets lightly with salt and pepper. Coat with a steak sauce of your choice. Cover the filets top and bottom with the lemon-and-herb spice blend. Heat a heavy-bottomed skillet with the olive oil and butter. Brown both sides of the fish for about 10 to 15 minutes total. Serve with the fig gravy.

Makes 4 servings

— COUSINS B & B

POULTRY AND PORK

Honey-Chili Oriental Fried Chicken

Here is a spicier version of the traditional fried chicken. The taste significantly changes this dish into a down-home gourmet preparation. A nice accompaniment to this dish is Elmo's jazzed up Spicy Three-Cheese Macaroni on page 111.

8   chicken breasts (with bone)
    Salt and pepper
1   cup all-purpose flour
1   pint cooking oil
2   tablespoons olive oil
⅓   cup water
1   tablespoon or so cornstarch
⅓   cup fresh lemon juice

4   teaspoons hot chili sesame oil
1½ tablespoons soy sauce
1   tablespoon grated fresh
    gingerroot
4   tablespoons honey
1   tablespoon minced garlic
8   scallions, finely chopped

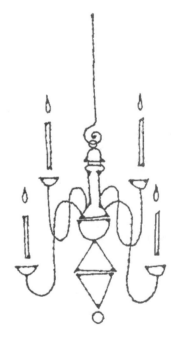

Season the chicken with salt and pepper to taste. Spoon the flour into a medium-sized plastic bag, add chicken, and shake until the chicken is well coated. Preheat a wok and add the cooking oil. When oil is hot, add the chicken and fry until golden brown. Drain and set aside.

Add the olive oil to the wok. Blend the water and cornstarch; set aside. When olive oil is hot, add the lemon juice, sesame oil, soy sauce, ginger, honey, garlic, and scallions. Pour in the cornstarch mixture. Season with salt and pepper. Add the chicken to the wok. Place the lid on the wok and simmer for about 10 to 15 minutes, or until the chicken is hot.

Makes 8 servings

— *COUSINS B & B*

Apple-Thyme Chicken

The folks in Julian, California, really know how to live, and this recipe proves it. Chicken deglazed with that old apple brandy known as Calvados and some pure apple cider from the hilly orchards, is testimony to a good time in this western city just outside San Diego.

¼ cup butter
4 tablespoons fresh thyme, finely chopped, plus a little more for garnish
6 skinless, boneless chicken breasts
3 tart apples, cored, peeled, and cut into medium-thick wedges

2 tablespoons sugar
½ cup apple juice
3 tablespoons Calvados
½ cup heavy cream
   Kosher salt and white pepper

In a large sauté pan, melt the butter over medium-high heat. Add the thyme and the chicken breasts. Sauté the chicken until it is golden brown, about 4 to 5 minutes on each side. Place the chicken on a plate and keep warm in the oven.

Return the pan to the heat and add the apples, cooking just a few minutes to soften. Transfer the apples to a plate and sprinkle them with the sugar.

Pour the apple juice into the pan and deglaze. Pour the brandy into a small saucepan and ignite. Add to the deglazed pan juices. Strain into a saucepan and simmer until just slightly reduced. Add the cream and season with salt and pepper.

Ladle a spoonful of the sauce into a serving dish. Place the chicken breasts on top. Pour another scant ladle of the sauce on top of the chicken breast. Top with apples and finish with a sprinkling of thyme.

Makes 6 servings

— *ORCHARD HILL COUNTRY INN*

Saffron-and-Honey-Glazed Medieval Baked Chicken

During the Middle Ages, cooks used a lot of fruits and nuts in their every-day savory cooking. This traditional old-English recipe, called also Henne Dorre or Golden Chicken, is a festive and easy dish to prepare for com-pany. Gilding the chicken, or glazing it with saffron, was a medieval tra-dition, as they liked to make everything festive, including their food. And so it continues on at Ravenwood.

CHICKEN
¼ cup walnuts, coarsely chopped
¼ cup slivered almonds
2 tablespoons butter, plus more for rubbing
3 apples, cored, peeled, and cut into small dice
⅔ cup golden raisins
½ cup currants
½ **teaspoon ground cinnamon**
¼ teaspoon fresh rosemary, finely crushed
1 large roasting chicken, giblets removed

GLAZE
6 egg yolks
⅛ teaspoon saffron or turmeric
2 tablespoons honey

GARNISH
Assortment of dried fruits and nuts
Parsley

Preheat the oven to 350°. Sauté the nuts in the butter for just a few seconds. Add the apples, raisins, and currants, and sprinkle in the spices. Stuff the nuts-and-fruits mixture into the chicken cavity. Rub the skin with butter or oil. Bake the stuffed chicken for 1½ to 2 hours, or until fork tender. Remove the chicken from the oven and turn the temperature up to 400°.

Prepare the glaze. Beat the eggs with the saffron and honey just lightly to incorporate. Use a brush to coat all parts of the bird with the glaze. Return the chicken to the oven and bake for 5 to 7 minutes to set the glaze. Serve on a platter garnished with dried fruits and nuts and some parsley.

Makes 4 servings

— *RAVENWOOD CASTLE*

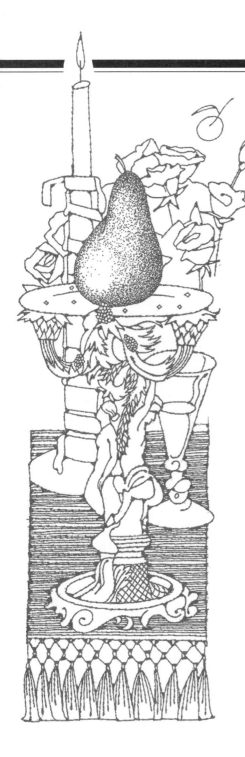

Peach Chutney with Tarragon Chicken

Sweet to tangy flavors pair well with the woodsy taste of the marinated and grilled chicken.

MARINADE
- 3 cloves garlic, finely chopped
- ½ tablespoon dried tarragon
- 1 sprig fresh tarragon, finely chopped
- ¼ cup olive oil
- 1 tablespoon fresh lemon juice
- 1 teaspoon Kosher salt
- 1 teaspoon coarsely ground black pepper
- 6 large chicken breasts, fat trimmed

CHUTNEY
- 2 cups cider vinegar
- 2 cups sugar
- 1 tablespoon butter
- 2 pounds fresh peaches, peeled and chopped
- 3 tablespoons triple-sec liqueur
- ½ cup brown sugar
- 2 tablespoons finely chopped fresh ginger
- 5 cloves garlic, finely chopped
- 1½ teaspoons salt
- 1½ cups golden raisins
- 2 tablespoons mustard seeds

ASSEMBLY
- 2 sprigs fresh tarragon, chopped for garnish

Combine all of the ingredients for the marinade and place the chicken with the marinade into a baking dish. Marinate in the refrigerator for 3 to 4 hours. Prepare the chutney.

In a medium saucepan, combine the vinegar and the white sugar and boil until a thick syrup forms, about 45 minutes to an hour or more.

When the liquid turns to a syrup, melt the butter over medium-high heat in a large sauté pan, add the peaches and sauté until soft. Turn the heat up and add the liqueur. Boil for a moment and then remove the pan from the heat.

Add the peach mixture to the syrup. Mix well to incorporate and then add the brown sugar, ginger, garlic, salt, raisins, and mustard seeds. Cook over low heat for about 30 minutes.

Remove the chicken from the refrigerator and grill until a light golden brown. (Finish in the oven, if necessary.)

To serve, place a chicken breast onto an individual serving plate. Add a few teaspoons of the chutney, draped over the chicken. Sprinkle fresh tarragon over the top.

(*Note:* There will be extra chutney as it makes about 2 quarts. Preserve in the refrigerator for future use.)

Makes 4 to 6 servings

— *THE NOTCHLAND INN*

Southwest Country-Style Rabbit Stew

The neighboring deserts of the Southwest provide the fresh flavors in this otherwise traditional French stew. The rabbit is braised and then set into a pot with a host of spices and red wine. Can't you just see the meat and colorful vegetables bubbling quietly on a stove in a country crock or quaint Dutch oven in a stone farmhouse, perhaps as the lavender sways in a field? The San Sophia Inn brings Provence ever so close with this excellent dish. Substitute chicken for the rabbit, if desired. The stew may be served with chips of deep-fried celery root. (See Celeriac Chips page 138.)

3 pounds rabbit or chicken legs and thighs
1 tablespoon ground cumin
½ teaspoon chili powder
½ teaspoon ground coriander
1 large clove garlic, minced
1 teaspoon cayenne pepper
Salt and pepper
1 cup all-purpose flour
2 tablespoons olive oil

½ large onion, coarsely diced
1 carrot, coarsely diced
2 ripe Roma tomatoes, cut into medium dice
¼ cup red wine
1 cup glace de viande (brown meat syrup available in gourmet food stores)
2 serrano chilies
Salt and pepper

Rub the meat with a mixture of the cumin, chili powder, coriander, garlic, and cayenne. Season with salt and pepper and sprinkle with the flour, coating all sides well.

In a large sauté pan, heat the oil until the pan is smoky hot. Brown the meat. Add the onion, carrot, and tomatoes and deglaze with the red wine. Reduce the mixture for approximately 45 minutes. Add the glace de viande and the chilies. Add enough water to almost cover the contents of the pot. Cover the pot and cook on the stove for 2 hours or in a preheated 400° oven.

(*Note:* About 45 minutes before ready, you may add 6 medium white potatoes, peeled and sliced into large ovals.)

Makes 4 servings

— *SAN SOPHIA INN*

Roasted Vegetable and Corn Milk Chili

Chef/innkeeper Elizabeth Turney offers an interesting twist to vegetarian chili by roasting the vegetables, introducing a sweet taste to the traditional dish. Elizabeth reports, "This is a great Saturday night supper-for-a-crowd recipe. I like to serve it with crusty bread or focaccia and a crunchy garden salad with grapefruit added to keep the palate cleansed." Elizabeth suggests roasting the vegetables on an outside grill to intensify their flavor with a smoky edge. The chili may be prepared a day ahead and just reheated.

BEANS
1 pound dried great northern, pinto, or kidney beans, soaked for 8 hours

VEGETABLES
6 plum tomatoes
4 ears corn
1 large onion
4 cloves garlic
2 jalapeño peppers, halved, seeded, and finely diced
1 tablespoon fresh or 1 teaspoon dried oregano
1 tablespoon fresh or 1 teaspoon dried basil
2 tablespoons olive oil
4 red bell peppers, quartered and seeded
1 teaspoon coarse salt

SOUP POT
1 tablespoon olive oil
½ teaspoon cayenne pepper
2 teaspoons ground cumin
½ tablespoon chili powder
3 cups chicken or vegetable broth
1 tablespoon tomato paste

Preheat the oven to 450° or heat the grill to high.

Prepare the vegetables. Halve the tomatoes, removing and reserving seeds and juice; cut into small dice. Remove the corn kernels from the ears, then scrape again to remove the milk from the husks and place whatever milk you can remove in a small dish. In a large baking dish, place the onion, tomatoes, garlic, jalapeños, oregano, and basil. Toss the vegetables with the corn milk and then with the olive oil. Season with the salt. Place bell peppers on top of the vegetables, skin side up, and place pan in the oven (or on the grill) for 30 minutes.

Vegetables are roasted when onions are translucent. Remove from the heat and peel the peppers, discarding blackened skins.

While the vegetables roast, place a stockpot over medium-high heat and heat the olive oil, adding the cayenne, cumin, and chili powder. Stir for about 1 minute until aromatic. Add the broth and beans and bring to a simmer. Add the roasted vegetables, tomato seeds and juice, and tomato paste. When peppers are cooled, remove their seeds, chop peppers coarsely, and add to the pot.

Let the stew simmer, covered, for at least 1½ hours. If too thin, remove the lid and allow the steam to escape. Chili will thicken as it continues to simmer. Season with salt and pepper. Serve with a choice of toppings such as cooked ground sausage, cheese, guacamole, and sour cream.

Makes 8 servings

— *BEAR CREEK LODGE*

Applewood-Smoked and Rosemary Cornish Hens

Innkeeper and cook Neil Myers showed us on camera how we can smoke poultry right in our own kitchen without fancy smokers, but rather on the stove-top. Neil uses applewood because the inn is near an orchard. But hickory chips are more commercially available. Smoking time varies with the type of wood—less for a stronger flavor such as hickory, a little more for a subtler taste such as applewood. "The fun is to experiment until you get the degree of smoky flavor you like," says Neil. Besides the wood chips, all you need are 2 large disposable roasting pans and a kitchen baking rack. And there are more good things I love about this recipe—an apple slice and rosemary sprig tucked under the wing. The hens need to marinate for 4 hours or overnight.

3 large Cornish game hens

MARINADE
1 tablespoon finely minced
  rosemary
2 cloves garlic
1 shallot
2 tablespoons apple-cider
  vinegar
¼ cup olive oil
1 can (12 ounces) frozen apple
  juice concentrate
¾ cup water

SAUCE
4 cups apple cider
4 cups chicken stock, homemade preferred

1 clove garlic, minced
1 shallot, minced
1 sprig fresh rosemary, 6 inches
1 tablespoon honey
  Salt and pepper to taste
  Calvados brandy to taste
  Applewood chips or other
  suitable wood chips which
  have been soaked in water
  for at least 1 hour, enough
  to cover the bottom of 1 roasting pan

GARNISH
1 red apple
6 sprigs fresh rosemary, 2 inches

Begin by marinating the hens. Process minced rosemary, garlic cloves, and the shallot until chopped, a few turns. Add the vinegar and oil and process again. Add the apple juice concentrate and the water and process again. Set aside.

Cut the hens into halves with kitchen shears. Cut through the breastbone and then along both sides of the backbone, thereby removing the backbone, tail, and any remainder of the neck. Trim any excess skin or fat. Wash hens carefully to remove any bone slivers. Pat dry. Pour the marinade over the hen halves to coat all sides. Place in the refrigerator for 4 to 8 hours.

Meanwhile, prepare the sauce. Combine the cider and stock in a large skillet and cook over high heat until sauce reduces to about 3 cups, about 20 minutes. Transfer to a smaller skillet and add the garlic, shallot, rosemary, and honey, and continue cooking over medium heat until reduced to 1½ cups. Pour the mixture through a strainer, discarding the garlic, rosemary, and shallots. Season with salt and pepper and add 1 teaspoon Calvados or more if desired after tasting.

Preheat the oven to 375°. Place 1 disposable roasting pan over the front and back burners of the stovetop. Drain the wood chips and spread them over the bottom of the pan. Place a rack inside the pan, large enough to hold all of the hens. Arrange the hens, bone side down, evenly on the rack. Season with salt and pepper. Place the other pan upside down over the first to make a lid. Turn burners on to medium heat. Check every few minutes until smoke starts to form; time varies according to type and dryness of wood. As soon as smoke forms, set timer for 5 minutes. At the end of 5 minutes, remove the hens to a shallow roasting pan and place them in the oven for 30 minutes, or until juices run clear. If the skin is not brown enough, run under the broiler. To serve, garnish with an apple slice and rosemary sprig tucked under the wing. Pour warmed sauce over the bird.

Makes 6 servings

— *INN AT VAUCLUSE SPRING*

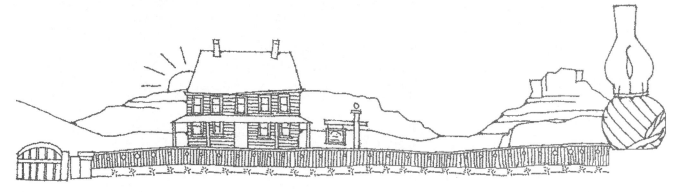

Chipotle Pork Tenderloin with Apple Tomatillo Sauce

Tomatillos are Mexican green ground cherries that have the flavor of lemon-apple herbs, so they complement the apples in the sauce. Tomatillos are available in many supermarkets and specialty stores, even in the Montana Bitterroot region where innkeeper/chef Elizabeth Turney finds them. The pork is marinated in the chipotle (chili) peppers with sugar, honey, and Cilantro. The tenderloins are then broiled to sear. You can start the sauce and the marinade a day ahead of serving time, but you will need to begin to prepare the tenderloins 3 hours ahead of time.

MARINADE
- 2 small chipotle peppers in sauce
- 1 small bunch Cilantro
- ¼ cup brown sugar
- ¼ cup honey

SAUCE
- 10 tomatillos
- 1 medium onion, cut into large dice
- 3 cloves garlic
- 1 large apple, cored and sliced
- 1 tablespoon cooking oil
- 1 tablespoon sugar
- 1 tablespoon Calvados brandy, optional

PORK
- 1½ tablespoons olive oil
- 1 large onion, thinly sliced
- 2 pork tenderloins, about 3 pounds
- ½ cup chicken broth
- ½ cup rum
- ¼ cup apple cider vinegar
- 2 tablespoons half-and-half

Combine the marinade ingredients in a food processor and blend until smooth. Two hours before cooking, spread the marinade over the pork tenderloins in a baking dish. Cover and refrigerate.

Begin by making the sauce. Preheat the oven to 425°. In a medium-sized roasting pan, toss together the tomatillos, diced onion, garlic, and apple with the cooking oil to coat and then sprinkle with the sugar. Place in the oven for 20 to 30 minutes until the tomatillos pop their skins but are still green and the onion is translucent. Remove from the oven and mix in the Calvados. Pour the mixture into a food processor and blend until puréed. Set aside.

When ready to cook, preheat the broiler. Heat the olive oil in a skillet and sauté the sliced onion until tender. Transfer onion to the roasting pan with the pork and add the broth, rum, and vinegar. Place the pan on the second rack in the broiler and broil for 10 minutes, turning the tenderloins. Turn the broiler off and heat the oven to 375°. Cook the meat for about another 20 to 30 minutes, turning the pork once and letting it cook until barely pink. Remove the pork from the pan and cover loosely with foil to keep warm. Place the roasting pan with the onion on a medium-high burner and add the half- and-half, stirring to combine. Slice the tenderloins and top with the onion. Spoon the sauce over all.

Makes 6 servings

— *BEAR CREEK LODGE*

BEEF, VEAL, LAMB

Easy Company's-Coming Beef in Puff Pastry

New cook or advanced, this is one of those great dishes you can always count on to make entertaining simple and elegant. Chef Scott Brouse uses a quality tender beef and adds caramelized onions and a delicate sauce to complete the dish. A surprise awaits as you bite into the pastry-crusted beef to find the mellow texture and the pungent palate teaser of Stilton cheese.

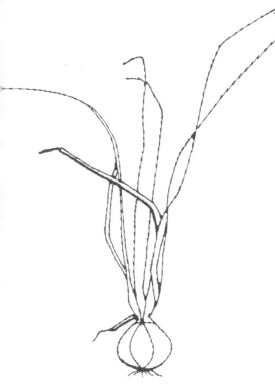

1 filet of beef, 3 pounds	SAUCE
¼ cup brandy	¼ cup (½ stick) butter
¼ cup (½ stick) butter, melted	⅔ cup finely diced onions
1 cup diced portobello mush-rooms, without stems	2 tablespoons sugar
Salt and pepper	½ cup dry sherry
2 ounces dry white wine	⅛ teaspoon thyme
1 sheet puff pastry, 12 inches square	¼ teaspoon chives
Flour	2 cups beef stock
1 cup Stilton cheese, crumbled (substitute with blue cheese)	1½ tablespoons cornstarch
3 egg whites, for egg wash	1½ tablespoons cold water

Preheat the oven to 425°. Place the beef on a 12-inch roasting pan and bake until the internal temperature reaches 120°, approximately 20 minutes. After baking, place the beef in a sauté pan over high heat and flambé with the brandy, half at a time. Remove the beef from the pan and allow to cool at room temperature.

Pour the melted butter into a medium-sized sauté pan and sauté the mushrooms for 2 minutes, seasoning with salt and pepper. Add the wine and cook for 2 more minutes. Remove the mushrooms from the heat and set aside.

Place the sheet of pastry on a level surface. Lightly dust the pastry with the flour. Evenly spread the mushroom mixture over the top, leaving a 2-inch border around the pastry. Evenly spread the cheese over the mushrooms. Carefully place the beef over the cheese along an edge of the pastry. Carefully roll the filet with the pastry. Seal the rolled edge with egg whites and gently tuck under the beef. Grease a baking sheet and place the wrapped beef, seam side down, on the baking sheet. Bake for 10 minutes and then turn the oven down to 375°. Bake for another 20 minutes, or until the pastry is golden brown. Remove and let stand for 15 minutes before slicing and serving.

During the latter half of the baking time, prepare the sauce. In a medium-sized sauté pan, melt the butter and sauté the onions and sugar constantly until they turn golden brown. Add the sherry, thyme, and chives and cook for 5 minutes, until the alcohol is evaporated. Add the stock and simmer on low heat for 10 minutes. Mix the water and cornstarch and add to the cooking sauce a little at a time, until the sauce thickens. (Use only enough cornstarch until the sauce coats the back of a spoon.) Remove the sauce from the heat and serve with slices of the pastry-crusted beef.

Makes 6 servings

— *INN AT OLDE NEW BERLIN*

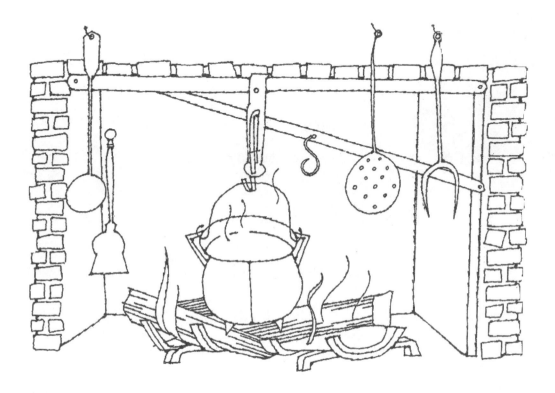

Filet of Elk with Red Currant Sauce

The Davy Jackson is a bed and breakfast, but occasionally dinner is served. One of the most acclaimed meals features this recipe. Elk is the meat of choice out on the range in Wyoming, although it is mostly farmed and imported from New Zealand. Indeed, elk is tender when cooked the innkeeper's way described here, and you will find this a delight to serve. Substitute with venison. Since elk is so lean, bacon fat is added to the cooking process to prevent dryness and further tenderize the meat. Begin recipe preparations a day in advance. There are many recipes for sauce espagñole but innkeeper Kay Minns has her own version here that has a light flavor.

(Note: Extra sauce may be frozen. The buttermilk reduces the wild taste of the game.)

MARINADE
- 4 elk tenderloin steaks, each 6 to 8 ounces, or substitute with venison
- 1 cup buttermilk

SAUCE ESPAGÑOLE
- 1 ham hock or veal bone
- 4 tablespoons butter
- 1 large carrot, coarsely diced
- 1 large onion, coarsely diced
- 2 ribs celery, coarsely diced
- 1 turnip or parsnip, coarsely diced
- ½ cup coarsely diced tomatoes
- ½ cup all-purpose flour
- 2 quarts brown stock
- ½ cup red wine
- 1 sprig fresh thyme
- 2 bay leaves

RED CURRANT SAUCE
- 2 tablespoons red currant jelly
- 6 tablespoons heavy cream
- 1¼ cups sauce espagnole

ASSEMBLY
- ¼ pound bacon, cut into thin strips
  Freshly ground pepper and salt
- 4 tablespoons butter

Trim the steaks carefully to remove any visible fat. Place the steaks in a glass dish and add the buttermilk. Marinate the elk in the refrigerator overnight.

Meanwhile, prepare the sauce espagñole. Brown the ham hock or veal bone in a large pan. Add the butter and all of the diced vegetables. Sprinkle the flour over the vegetables and stir until the flour is

incorporated. Add the brown stock, red wine, thyme, and bay leaves; bring to a boil, stirring constantly. Reduce the heat and simmer sauce for 3 to 4 hours. Turn off the heat and cool the sauce. Strain the sauce into another dish and refrigerate overnight. Remove the layer of fat, and remove and discard the bay leaves.

Prepare the currant sauce. Melt the jelly and stir in the cream. Add this to the sauce espagñole.

When ready to serve, remove the steaks from the buttermilk and pat dry with a towel. Add the bacon to the steaks, by placing on top. Season with salt and pepper and fry in the butter until lightly browned. Elk should be served rare or medium rare inside. Heat the red currant sauce and serve over the elk.

Makes 4 servings

— *THE DAVY JACKSON INN*

Lamb with Roasted-Garlic-Beet Risotto

The lamb is wrapped in Italian ham and encrusted with black pepper. This is a nice Saturday-night special for the family, and it is a cinch to make.

RISOTTO
- ¼ cup olive oil
- ¼ cup finely diced Vidalia onion
- 1 cup diced fresh beets
  Salt and pepper to taste
- 1 cup Arborio rice
- 3 cups chicken stock
- ½ cup Parmesan cheese
- 30 cloves garlic, roasted (see page 137 on garlic roasting), finely chopped
- ¼ cup fresh basil, cut into julienne

LAMB
- 4 lamb loins, each 6 to 8 ounces, trimmed
- ¼ cup olive oil
  Ground black pepper
- 8 slices prosciutto

GARNISH
  Assortment of chopped fresh herbs

Begin by making the risotto. Heat the olive oil over medium-high heat in a medium-sized nonstick saucepan and sauté the onion until translucent. Add the beets and season with salt and pepper. Add the uncooked rice and coat well with the olive oil and onion. Stir in the chicken broth in thirds, stirring constantly until the rice is almost dry before adding the next third and so on. Rice should be cooked *al dente*. Remove from the heat and add the cheese, roasted garlic cloves, and basil. Keep warm and prepare the lamb.

Preheat the oven to 400°. Brush the lamb with olive oil and sprinkle both sides with a generous amount of cracked pepper. Wrap each loin with a slice of prosciutto. Heat a medium-sized nonstick sauté pan and brush with olive oil. Place the wrapped lamb in the pan and brown on all sides. Place in a baking dish and bake for 5 to 8 minutes, or until the insides of the lamb are just slightly pink. Remove from the heat and let rest. While the lamb rests, spoon risotto onto the center of each plate. Cut the lamb loins crosswise into ¾- to 1-inch medallions and place around or on top of the risotto. Sprinkle with fresh herbs.

Makes 4 servings

— THE INN AT MONTCHANIN VILLAGE

Ragout of Lamb with Garden Vegetables

Preparation time is 2 hours for this cornucopia of herbs, vegetables, and tender lamb. You just need to prepare the vegetables. The rest of it is up to the stew to cook away and let the flavors meld.

LAMB
- 2 tablespoons cooking oil
- 2 pounds lamb shoulder, trimmed of any fat, cut into 2-ounce cubes
- 2 pounds lamb short ribs
  Salt and pepper
- 1 teaspoon sugar
- 3 tablespoons all-purpose flour
- 4 tomatoes, peeled, seeded, and cut into bite-size pieces
- 2 garlic cloves, crushed
- 1 *bouquet garni* comprised of 2 sprigs parsley, 1 bay leaf, 2 basil leaves, 1 sprig rosemary, 2 sprigs thyme, all tied in a small mesh bag
- 2 quarts lamb stock or water

VEGETABLES
- 1 cup fresh English peas
- 8 ounces green beans, cut into 1½-inch pieces
- 8 ounces fresh asparagus tips
- 4 tablespoons butter
- 2 tablespoons sugar
  Salt and pepper to taste
- 16 baby turnips, peeled
- 16 pearl onions, peeled
- 16 baby carrots, peeled
- 8 small new potatoes, peeled
- 8 ounces cherry tomatoes

Preheat the oven to 350°. Spoon the oil into a large nonreactive casserole dish over medium-high heat. Add all of the lamb and season with salt and pepper. Add the sugar and let the meat brown on all sides. When meat is browned, drain the fat from the pan and add the flour, cooking for about 1 minute. Add the tomatoes, garlic, *bouquet garni,* and the lamb stock or water, just enough to cover the meat. Cover with a lid and cook for 1 hour.

Meanwhile, prepare the vegetables. Blanch the peas, green beans, and asparagus for 2 minutes in boiling salted water. Refresh with iced water; set aside. Place the butter, sugar, salt, pepper, turnips, onions, and carrots into a large sauté pan and cook over medium-high heat for 3 minutes. Add to the casserole with the potatoes. Simmer for ½ hour. Season the casserole with salt and pepper. Add the peas, green beans, asparagus, and cherry tomatoes, and cook for another 15 minutes. Remove the *bouquet garni,* and the stew is ready for serving.

Makes 8 servings

— *THE PLANTATION INN/GERARD'S RESTAURANT*

107

Native-American Lamb Posole

Posole* *is a southwestern dish taught to innkeeper Ava Bowers by her native New Mexican friends. A hearty soup, Ava says that when she cooks this, traditionally during winter holidays, the aromas fill the inn and guests say they can smell it for miles around. Hmmm, what is in this dish anyway?! Ava uses lamb in her* posole, *but you may substitute pork or beef instead.*

5 chili pods, stems and seeds removed, pods rinsed
1½ pounds lean lamb, cut into bite-size pieces and seared
3 cups frozen *posole,* washed
2½ quarts water
2 medium-sized onions, cut into ½-inch dice

4 cloves garlic, minced
3 teaspoons granulated garlic
2½ teaspoons salt
12 ounces red chili purée
2 tablespoons finely chopped fresh cilantro

Place the chili pods, lamb, and the *posole* into a pot of the water. Bring to a slow boil, cover, and turn down the heat. Simmer for 30 minutes. Add the onions, both forms of garlic, the salt, and the chili purée. Add more water if needed to keep somewhat soupy.

Turn the heat up again and bring to a boil. Cover and cook over medium-low heat for 2½ hours until tender.

Sprinkle with cilantro just before cooking time ends.

Makes 8 to 10 servings

— *APACHE CANYON RANCH*

*Posole *is a specially grown large-kernel corn that pops open while cooking. It has many of the qualities of hominy.*

Side Dishes

Toasted Noodle and Rice Pilaf

The pilaf is often served with the Apple-Thyme Chicken on page 92. This is one of the inn's most requested recipes and a bit unusual with the inclusion of noodles with the rice.

5 cups chicken broth, plus enough water to make 6 cups total	2 cups golden raisins, plumped in hot water and drained
1½ cups (3 sticks) butter	¾ cup toasted whole blanched almonds
2 cups uncooked rice	
3 cups fine uncooked egg noodles, toasted in the oven for about 12 minutes (watch carefully)	

In a medium saucepan over high heat, bring the broth and the water to a boil. Add 6 tablespoons of the butter and all of the rice. Cover the pan and turn the heat down to a simmer. Simmer for 15 minutes. Add the toasted noodles. Cover and simmer for an additional 10 minutes until the rice and noodles are tender; add more broth or water if necessary; set aside.

Melt the remaining butter and sauté the plumped raisins and toasted almonds just until the raisins are lightly browned. Mix in with the rice and noodles and serve.

Makes 8 to 10 servings

— *ORCHARD HILL COUNTRY INN*

Wild Wyoming Potato-and-Vegetable Compote

The mashed potatoes in this dish help hold together layers of vegetables as though you were building a torte. Another name for this recipe could be a potato-and-vegetable layer cake.

POTATOES
- 6 large white russet potatoes, 4½ to 5 pounds
- ½ cup milk

VEGETABLES
- 1½ pounds thin asparagus spears
- 6 to 8 cabbage leaves
- 1 red bell pepper, chopped
- 1 cup green peas
- 1 small zucchini, sliced
- 8 sprigs chives
- ½ cup (1 stick) butter, softened

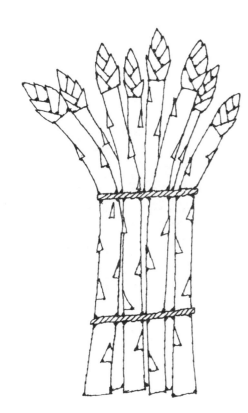

Peel the potatoes and cut them into medium-size pieces. Place in a pot with enough water to cover the potatoes by 1 inch or so. Boil the potatoes until tender, drain, and place in a mixing bowl with the milk. Gently mash the potatoes and milk together. Set the potatoes aside until cool. It is very important to cool all the ingredients before building the compote.

Wash and drain the asparagus, snapping off all but 3 inches, discarding the tough, woody ends. The asparagus should be cut to the height of a 2-quart soufflé dish that is 3 to 4 inches tall. Blanch the asparagus for 1 minute, drain, and cool with cold water. Place on paper towels to dry. Set aside.

Place the cabbage leaves in boiling water and cook for approximately 6 minutes, or until soft. Drain and cool, place on paper towels, and set aside.

Cut the red bell pepper into thin strips; blanch, drain, and cool. Blanch green peas, drain, and set aside. Slice the zucchini into ¼-inch disks; blanch, drain, and let cool.

Preheat the oven to 350°. Butter the soufflé dish, heavier on the sides (this is the *mortar* that will hold up your asparagus). Stick asparagus to the side of the dish, tips down, all the way around the dish. On the bottom place the red pepper, zucchini, and chives. Set aside any vegetables you do not use for the final presentation.

Add half of the cooled mashed potatoes. Make a slight indent in the center and move more potatoes to the side. Place half of the cabbage leaves in the indent. Pour the green peas into the cabbage. Place

the remainder of the cabbage over top of the peas, creating a pocket in the potatoes. Add the remainder of the potatoes and smooth out.

Bake for 45 minutes, or until all ingredients are hot. Remove from the oven and immediately place a serving dish over the soufflé dish. Flip over onto the serving dish. When ready to serve, cut the compote into wedges. Garnish with any leftover vegetables.

Makes 6 to 8 servings

— *THE DAVY JACKSON INN*

Spicy Three-Cheese Baked Macaroni

Here is a twist on the classic dish, using Cajun spice and an herbal bread stuffing.

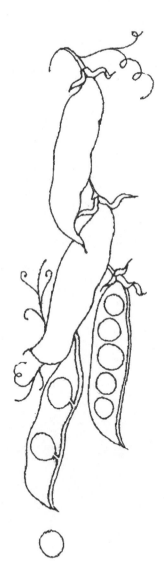

1 cup herbal stuffing, unprepared
3 eggs
2 teaspoons butter, melted
½ cup Parmesan cheese
½ cup milk
1 teaspoon Cajun spice
¼ teaspoon salt
2 cups shredded mozzarella cheese
2 cups extra-sharp cheddar cheese
2 cups elbow macaroni, cooked *al dente*

Preheat the oven to 350°.

Spray a baking dish 13 x 9 inches with nonstick cooking oil spray. Sprinkle the stuffing into the dish to form a crustlike base. Whisk together the eggs, butter, Parmesan cheese, milk, Cajun spice, salt, and mozzarella and cheddar cheeses. Add the cooked pasta to the baking dish. Pour the cheese mixture over the top and fold in the remainder of the stuffing. Bake for 30 to 45 minutes, or until the cheese bubbles.

Makes 6 to 8 servings

— *COUSINS B & B*

Couscous and Wild Rice Pancakes

A fun recipe to make, the pancakes are especially nice with the Barbecued, Marinated Trout with Onion-Caper Relish on page 82. The inn also serves them with a sweet duck breast or just with maple syrup as a brunch recipe. The couscous holds things together nicely and gives the pancakes added texture.

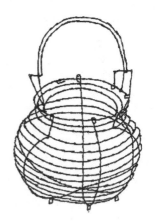

RICE
- 1 tablespoon olive oil
- ¼ cup minced shallots (2 tablespoons)
- 1 cup wild rice
- 1½ cups chicken or vegetable stock

PANCAKES
- ⅔ cup chicken stock
- 6 tablespoons couscous
- ¾ cup minced onion
- 1 tablespoon all-purpose flour
- 1 teaspoon salt
- ¼ teaspoon ground black pepper
- 3 eggs
- 1 tablespoon olive oil
- 1½ teaspoons hot chili oil

Using a small stockpot, heat the olive oil and sauté the shallots until translucent. Add the wild rice and cook for 2 minutes, stirring constantly. Add the stock, cover, and simmer for 45 minutes, or until the rice is tender.

Prepare the couscous. Bring the stock to a boil in a medium-sized saucepan. Stir in the couscous and return to a boil; then remove from the heat, cover, and set aside for 5 minutes. After 5 minutes, uncover and fluff with a fork. Set aside to cool.

In a large bowl, combine the cooked wild rice, onion, flour, salt, and pepper, mixing well. Lightly beat the eggs and add to the wild rice along with the couscous. Set aside.

Combine the olive oil and the hot chili oil. Brush a nonstick skillet with the oil mixture. Using a ¼ cup measure, place batter for 4 pancakes in the skillet, flattening the mixture with the back side of a spatula. Cook over medium heat until the pancake is firm and nicely browned, about 5 minutes. Turn and cook the other side for 3 minutes.

Continue with the remaining batter, oiling the pan when necessary. (You may hold the already-cooked pancakes in a warmed oven.)

Makes 4 to 6 servings

— *THE STEAMBOAT INN*

Roasted-Garlic Mashed Potatoes with Basil and Sun-Dried Tomatoes

Thyme & the River Too is one inn cookbook that is going to be around for a long time. The book is chockful of simple recipes that have great imagination and solidly good taste such as this delicious version of mashed potatoes.

2 pounds baking potatoes, peeled

2 tablespoons snipped sun-dried tomatoes, softened in hot water

¼ cup (½ stick) butter

¼ cup minced fresh basil

1 tablespoon mashed Roasted Garlic (see page 137)

4 to 6 tablespoons half-and-half

½ teaspoon salt

½ teaspoon ground black pepper

Boil the potatoes in lightly salted water until they are tender. When cooked, drain the potatoes and transfer to a mixing bowl. Add the tomatoes (drained), the butter, basil, and garlic. Beat to mix together. Add 4 tablespoons of the half-and-half, the salt, and the pepper. Add the additional half-and-half if the potatoes seem dry. Serve immediately.

Makes 6 to 8 servings

— *THE STEAMBOAT INN*

Red Bean Succotash

Reminiscent of the succotash prepared by early American settlers, this is a hearty and tasty dish suitable for any barbecue at your house.

3 ears corn
2 tablespoons butter
¼ medium onion, cut into a
   small dice
½ cup cooked red beans
½ cup cooked lima beans
1 medium zucchini, cut into
   thin ¼-inch slices

1 rehydrated ancho chili, stems
   and seeds removed and cut
   into ¼-inch dice
½ cup low-salt chicken stock
   Salt and pepper

Remove the kernels from the corn. In a medium saucepan, melt the butter and sauté the onion until translucent. Add the corn and cook for 5 minutes, stirring, over low heat. Add all of the beans, the zucchini, and the chili. Stir and add the stock. Cook the succotash over medium-low heat for about 15 minutes, until it is thoroughly heated through. Season with salt and pepper to taste.

Makes 2½ cups

— *THE CAPTAIN WHIDBEY INN*

Desserts

Buttermilk Pecan Pie

Most pecan pies are made with a thick corn syrup, but after much experimentation, Margaret Mosley found that buttermilk provides a nice custard base. Pecan pie is almost always in the oven at the plantation where pecan trees provide the nuts fresh from the trees.

CRUST
- 2 cups all-purpose flour
- 1 teaspoon salt
- ½ cup (1 stick) plus 2 tablespoons cold butter, cut into 1-inch pieces
- 2 tablespoons shortening
- ½ cup cold water

FILLING
- ½ cup (1 stick) butter
- 2 cups sugar
- 2 teaspoons vanilla extract
- 3 eggs
- 3 tablespoons all-purpose flour
- ¼ teaspoon salt
- 1 cup buttermilk
- ¾ cup to 1 cup toasted chopped pecans

Preheat the oven to 300°. Combine the flour and salt in a food processor. Cut in the cold butter and the shortening, pulsing to combine until the mixture resembles coarse meal. Slowly add the cold water through the feed tube until the dough forms a ball. Remove the dough and chill for about 1 hour.

Meanwhile, in a large bowl, cream together the butter and the sugar, adding the sugar gradually. Add the vanilla and then the eggs, one at a time. In a separate bowl, combine the flour and salt and add it to the sugar mixture. Stir in the buttermilk slowly.

Fit the chilled dough into a 9-inch tart pan with a removable bottom. Weigh down with beans or pie weights and bake in the oven for 5 to 8 minutes, or until slightly golden.

Sprinkle the toasted pecans over the bottom of the piecrust. Pour the custard batter over the pecans. Bake for 45 minutes to 1 hour, or until brown and set. You may serve the pie as is or drizzle with caramel sauce and top with a cherry or a whole pecan.

Makes 8 servings

— THE CEDARS PLANTATION

Tropical Fruit-Filled Pineapple with Meringue Topping

Chef Gerard Reversade uses pineapple shells as serving bowls for native island fruits that fill the pineapple. Ice cream and a sweet meringue top the fruit. Meringue desserts are making a comeback as they are so adaptable to almost any type of cuisine.

FRUIT
- 2 small pineapples
- 1 papaya, peeled, seeded, and cut into bite-size pieces
- 1 banana, cut into thin slices
- 1 small melon of choice, cut into balls
- 1 cup assorted berries of choice
- 1 star fruit, sliced
- 8 lychees
- 4 figs, each cut into 4 pieces
- 2 tablespoons sugar
- ¼ cup kirsch

MERINGUE
- 2 cups sugar
- 1 cup water
- 8 egg whites
- 1 teaspoon vanilla extract

ASSEMBLY
- 1 quart vanilla ice cream

Cut the pineapples into halves. Remove the cores and cut out the fruit, leaving the outsides intact to serve as bowls. Cut the pineapple into bite-size pieces.

Mix all of the fruits in a bowl with the sugar and Kirsch. Evenly divide among the 4 pineapple halves.

Preheat the oven to 400° and begin making the meringue. Heat the sugar and water in a small saucepan, cooking over medium-high heat until it reaches a hard boil and is thick and syrupy.

Meanwhile, whip the egg whites until they are stiff. Gradually add the syrup and then the vanilla, gently mixing into the egg whites.

Place the vanilla ice cream evenly over the fruits, then spread with a layer of meringue. Shovel the remaining meringue into a pastry bag fitted with a large star tip. Pipe stars on top of each pineapple. Bake in the oven for 5 to 8 minutes just until lightly browned. Serve at once.

Makes 4 servings

— *THE PLANTATION INN/GERARD'S RESTAURANT*

Sweet Marsala-Poached Pears with Amaretti Crunch

Simple desserts are perfect accompaniments to almost any meal. This recipe calls for ripe pears covered in a wine sauce with the texture of amaretti, airy Italian macaroon cookies made with almond paste. The pears are nice with a scoop of homemade ice cream such as peach or pistachio.

8 small Anjou pears
2 tablespoons fresh lemon juice
2 cups Marsala wine
3 tablespoons brown sugar
½ teaspoon ground cinnamon

¾ cup amaretti cookies, crushed

Preheat the oven to 350°. Cut a slice from the bottom of each pear so that it sits flat with its stem upright. Leave the skin and the stem intact. Brush each pear generously with the lemon juice. Set the pears in a baking dish 9 x 13 inches. Pour the wine over the pears, allowing the liquid to rest around the base of the fruit.

Combine the sugar and the cinnamon and sprinkle the mixture over the pears, followed by a sprinkling of the amaretti.

Bake the pears, uncovered, for 45 to 50 minutes, basting the fruit 3 or 4 times and cooking until the pears are tender. Serve warm at room temperature, spooning the wine sauce over the top.

Makes 8 servings

— *THE CAPTAIN FREEMAN INN*

Strawberry Swirl Cinnamon-Biscuit Pie

Most pies have a crust, but this old-fashioned dessert is all upper crust—in a manner of speaking—made of cinnamon pinwheels with strawberry jam. The pie plate is not lined with dough. The pie is visually inviting with its swirls of biscuits sitting on top of fresh-cooked strawberries.

FILLING
- 3 quarts fresh strawberries, hulled
- 1½ cups sugar
- 6 tablespoons cornstarch
- ⅔ cup water
- 1 tablespoon fresh lemon juice

BISCUITS
- 2 cups all-purpose flour
- ½ teaspoon salt
- 4 teaspoons baking powder
- ½ teaspoon cream of tartar
- 2 tablespoons sugar
- 1 tablespoon cinnamon
- ½ cup (1 stick) butter
- ⅔ cup milk
- ½ cup strawberry preserves
- 2 tablespoons or more cinnamon sugar for sprinkling

Place 2 quarts of the strawberries into a food processor. Pulse just a couple of times to crush the berries coarsely. (Do not over process.)

Add the berries to a large saucepan with the sugar, cornstarch, water, and lemon juice. Cook over medium heat until it jells, about 1 hour, or until the mixture is shiny. Slice the remaining berries and mix into the jelled filling.

Meanwhile, prepare the biscuits. In a large bowl, blend together all of the biscuit ingredients, except the preserves and cinnamon sugar. Using a pastry blender, blend the mixture into a thick dough with a clay-like texture.

Sprinkle a work surface with a little flour and roll out the dough to about ½-inch thick. Spread the top with the preserves, bringing it out close to the edge. (Only a thin layer is needed to fill the biscuit.) Sprinkle the preserves generously with cinnamon-sugar. Roll the dough up jelly-roll style, beginning at the wider side. Cut into ¼-inch slices. (Dough will be soft and appear not to hold its shape; however, the biscuits will rise and take shape during baking.) Set the biscuits aside.

When the filling is ready, remove from the stove and preheat the oven to 400°. Pour the prepared strawberry filling into a 9-inch greased deep-dish pie pan. Place the biscuits on top of the filling, around and in the center of the pan, about ½-inch apart.

Bake for 15 to 18 minutes or until filling is set and biscuits are golden brown. Cool pie to warm. Serve with sweetened whipped cream or ice cream, if desired.

(Note: There may be enough extra biscuit dough and filling for another smaller-size pie.)

Makes 6 to 8 servings

— THE NOTCHLAND INN

Sweet Potato Pie

A favorite from innkeeper Ava Bowers's southern roots, this pie is more often loaded with whole eggs and butter, but at the inn, Ava boasts that she has created a heart-healthy version that also tastes delicious.

2 medium-to-large sweet potatoes, peeled
2 egg whites
½ cup white sugar
1 cup brown sugar
½ cup freshly squeezed orange
juice
1 teaspoon vanilla or orange
extract
1 teaspoon grated nutmeg
1 teaspoon ground cinnamon
Grated rind of ½ orange
1 9-inch pie shell

Preheat the oven to 375°. Cut the sweet potatoes in large chunks and cook in water to cover until potatoes are tender when pierced with a fork.

While the potatoes cook, beat the egg whites and white sugar together until stiff peaks form; set aside. Mash the softened potatoes with a hand mixer on low to medium speed; add beaten egg whites, brown sugar, orange juice, vanilla, nutmeg, cinnamon, and orange rind. Mix with a hand mixer until very smooth. Pour into a prepared pie shell and bake for 1 hour, or until pie is set and slightly browned.

Makes 6 to 8 servings

— APACHE CANYON RANCH

Raspberry Coulis Cloud

The inn's version of a French classic dessert called oeufs à la neige, *this easy dessert is complete with finely spun caramel over puffy meringue mounds like clouds in a summer sky above a field of raspberries.*

BASE
1 cup cold milk
6 egg yolks
3 tablespoons all-purpose flour
5 tablespoons cornstarch
¾ cup sugar
1 cup hot milk
1 teaspoon vanilla extract
¾ cup heavy cream, whipped to
  stiff peaks

COULIS
½ cup frozen raspberries
1 tablespoon cassis
2 tablespoons sugar
  Additional fresh raspberries

MERINGUE
3 egg whites
⅛ teaspoon salt
½ cup sugar

CARAMEL
½ cup sugar
4 tablespoons water
1 tablespoon corn syrup

Begin by making the cream base. In a medium-sized mixing bowl, combine egg yolks, flour, cornstarch, and sugar. Then add cold milk and beat all together with a wire whisk until smooth. Add the hot milk, stirring constantly with the whisk. Transfer the mixture to a double boiler and cook over medium heat, stirring constantly with the whisk until a custard forms and thickens. Strain if necessary. Place the pan in a bowl of ice water and add the vanilla, stirring occasionally until the mixture cools. Refrigerate for 2 to 3 hours, until set. Remove from the refrigerator and whisk in the whipped heavy cream. Keep refrigerated while you prepare the coulis.

Place all of the coulis ingredients into the bowl of a food processor and process into a purée. Strain through a fine sieve to remove all of the seeds. Set aside while you prepare the meringue.

Beat the egg whites with the salt until stiff peaks form. Gradually beat in the sugar until the whites are stiff, glossy, and smooth. In a deep 12-inch skillet, pour water to the depth of 1 inch and place over high heat. Bring to a boil and reduce to a simmer. Scoop or pipe the meringue and carefully transfer the rounded scoops to the simmering water and cook for 2 minutes on each side, turning with 2 spoons. Lift the meringues with a slotted spoon onto a paper-towel-lined tray and allow to cool.

To assemble, swirl the coulis through the custard (do not over-mix). Pour all into glass dessert dishes layered with fresh raspberries. Top with a meringue cloud.

Prepare the caramel. In a heavy saucepan, combine the sugar, water, and corn syrup. Bring to a boil over high heat. Do not stir. Cover the pan to allow the steam to dissolve any crystals that may form. Uncover the pan and boil for several more minutes until the syrup is hazelnut brown. Watch carefully so that the syrup does not become too dark. Remove from the heat and let the caramel cool slightly. When it has become thick and syrupy, use a fork to drizzle over the meringues in fine, hairlike strands. Serve immediately.

Makes 4 servings

— *INN AT VAUCLUSE SPRING*

Hazelnut Orange Shortcake with Blueberry Sauce

The slightly sweet orange biscuit is a perfect partner for the blueberries and a nice change from the usual shortcake dessert with strawberries that is made as a layer cake. The biscuits add an interesting texture.

1¾ cups all-purpose flour
1 tablespoon baking powder
1 tablespoon sugar
½ teaspoon salt
½ cup finely chopped hazelnuts
1 tablespoon grated orange rind, plus peel of 1 whole orange
½ cup (1 stick) cold butter, cut into chunks
1 egg

½ cup whipping cream
2 tablespoons orange liqueur
1 quart blueberries, freshly preferred, plus a few more for garnish
¼ cup sugar
¼ cup corn syrup (2 tablespoons)
½ teaspoon grated nutmeg
Whipped cream for garnish, if desired

Preheat the oven to 425°. In a large bowl, mix together the flour, baking powder, sugar, salt, and nuts. Stir in the 1 tablespoon of orange rind. Cut in the butter until the mixture resembles coarse crumbs. Combine the egg, cream, and orange liqueur and add to the flour mixture. Stir just until the mixture begins to hold together. Turn onto a floured surface and knead 2 swift strokes to bind the dough. Using a rolling pin or your hands, flatten the dough to ½-inch thick. Cut out 10 biscuits with a 3-inch biscuit cutter and place them on ungreased baking sheet(s). Bake for 15 to 20 minutes, or until the tops start to brown.

While the biscuits are baking, crush half of the blueberries in a medium-sized saucepan. Add the remaining whole berries, sugar, corn syrup, peel of the whole orange, and the nutmeg. Cook over medium-high heat until thickened, stirring frequently. Remove the orange peel.

Cut each of the biscuits into halves and place one half on an individual serving plate. Cover with the warm blueberry mixture. Top with the remaining half of the biscuit and more berries. Garnish with extra fresh berries and whipped cream, if desired.

Makes 10 servings

— *THE STEAMBOAT INN*

Oliebollen

In the Pacific Northwest this old-time Dutch dessert is a favorite.

3 eggs, beaten
3 cups milk
¾ cup sugar
6 cups all-purpose flour
6 teaspoons baking powder
2 teaspoons salt
1½ teaspoons ground cinnamon
¼ teaspoon ground cloves

1½ cups currants
3 cups grated green apple
(about 3 apples)
3 tablespoons melted butter
Oil for deep-frying
½ cup or more cinnamon-sugar
mixture

In a medium mixing bowl, combine the eggs, milk, and sugar. In a larger bowl, combine the flour, baking powder, salt, cinnamon, and cloves. Add the wet ingredients to the dry ingredients and mix to combine. Fold in the currants, the apples, and the butter.

Pour enough oil into a large heavy-bottomed pan to reach a depth of 1½ inches. Heat the oil; it should be hot enough to sizzle when a ball is dropped into it. Using a cookie scoop, drop the balls into the pan and fry until brown on both sides. Turn balls onto paper towels to drain and dust with the cinnamon-sugar mixture. Cool down and serve or freeze.

Makes about 120

— *THE CAPTAIN WHIDBEY INN*

Pecan Beignets with Praline Sauce

Café Du Monde in New Orleans is said to be responsible for the preservation of beignets, soft, pillowlike doughnuts that are served with café au lait. These tasty little cakes are served at the Inn at Le Rosier gourmet style with homemade ice cream and a southern sauce by Chef Hallman Woods III. The beignets are fun to make and may even be served just with a cup of coffee in the morning. If you want to take the shortcut, you may be able to find a beignet mix in gourmet food shops and some grocery stores. Then prepare Chef Woods's praline sauce and add ice cream of your choice.

BEIGNETS
¼ cup lukewarm water
1 package active dry yeast
¼ cup sugar
2 tablespoons vegetable shortening
½ teaspoon salt
½ cup boiling water
½ cup heavy cream
1 egg, lightly beaten
4 to 4½ cups unsifted all-purpose flour
  Vegetable oil for deep-frying
  Powdered sugar for dusting

SAUCE
1 cup brown sugar
½ cup molasses
½ cup (1 stick) butter
¼ cup bourbon
1 cup roasted chopped pecans, plus pecans for garnish
  Ice cream

Pour the water into a shallow bowl and sprinkle the yeast over it. Let the yeast rest for 2 to 3 minutes, then mix well. Set in a warm, draft-free place for about 10 minutes, or until the yeast bubbles up and the mixture almost doubles in bulk.

Meanwhile, combine the sugar, the shortening, and the salt into a large mixing bowl. Pour in the boiling water and stir with a wooden spoon until the ingredients are thoroughly blended and the mixture has cooled to lukewarm. Stir in the heavy cream, the yeast mixture, and the egg. Add 2 cups of the flour. When it is completely incorporated, beat in up to 2½ cups more of the flour, ¼ cup at a time. Add only enough flour to make the dough smooth and not sticky. When

the dough becomes too stiff to stir easily with a spoon, work in the additional flour with your fingers.

Pour vegetable oil into a deep-fryer or large heavy saucepan to a depth of 2 to 3 inches and heat the oil until it reaches a temperature of 360° (test with thermometer; oil must be hot enough to sizzle right away when food is added).

Gather the dough into a ball, place it on a lightly floured surface and pat it into a rectangle about 1-inch thick. Dust a little flour over and under the dough and roll it out from the center to within an inch of the far edge. Lift the dough and turn it at right angles, then roll again from the center as before. Repeat—lifting, turning, rolling—until the rectangle is about ¼-inch thick and measures at least 25 x 10 inches. If dough sticks to the board, lift it with a wide metal spatula and sprinkle a little more flour underneath.

With a pastry wheel or sharp knife, cut the dough into 10 beignets, each 5 inches square, and deep-fry immediately, dropping the beignets 2 or 3 at a time into the hot oil. Turn them over with a slotted spoon as soon as they rise to the surface. Continue frying, turning the beignets frequently for about 3 to 5 minutes, or until they are crisp and golden brown on all sides. As they brown, transfer the beignets to paper towels to drain. They may be held in a warm oven for 15 minutes.

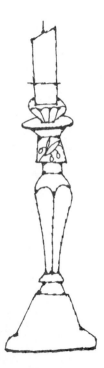

While the beignets stay warm, prepare the sauce. Melt the brown sugar, molasses, butter, and bourbon in a double boiler. When the mixture comes to a boil, add the roasted pecans. The sauce may be served warm at this point or held in the double boiler. (The sauce also holds well in advance in the refrigerator.)

To assemble the dessert, place one beignet on an individual dessert plate. Place a scoop of ice cream on the beignet. Working somewhat quickly to avoid undue melting, drizzle ample amounts of sauce over the ice cream and beignet. Sprinkle with additional pecans and serve immediately.

Makes 10 beignets, 5 inches square

— *INN AT LE ROSIER*

Almond Cookie Baskets for Peaches and Raspberry Sorbet

Wrap a warm, thin almond cookie around the base of a cup or glass, and in an instant you have an edible serving vessel for sorbet, ice cream, pudding, you name it. Here, Chef Scott Daniels gives us the how-to for making two types of sorbet. (See also Miss Scarlett's Sorbet on page 144, or make or buy your own favorite flavor.) This is such an easy dessert and yet so elegant. The cookie dough needs to set in the refrigerator a day before serving.

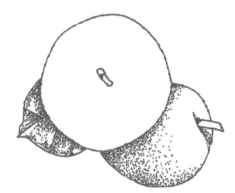

PEACH SORBET
1 cup puréed peeled fresh peaches (may substitute mangoes)
½ cup water
½ cup sugar
½ teaspoon freshly squeezed lemon juice

RASPBERRY SORBET
1 cup raspberry purée (strain out seeds)
½ cup sugar
½ cup water
½ teaspoon lemon juice

COOKIES
¾ cup blanched almonds
½ tablespoon all-purpose flour
1 cup sugar
Water to bind

GARNISH
Whole raspberries
Powdered sugar

To make each sorbet separately, combine the fruit purée with the water, sugar, and lemon juice. Mix well. Strain seeds through a cheesecloth and reserve ¾ cup of the raspberry purée for plate presentation. Freeze the rest in an electric ice-cream maker. Or simply boil the sugar and water until the sugar dissolves; mix with the other ingredients and cool, then pour into a container and freeze.

While the sorbet freezes, make the cookies. In a food processor, pulse the almonds with the flour and sugar until coarse. Slowly add the water, a tablespoon or so at a time, just until the mixture is puréed. Cover and let set in the refrigerator overnight. Line a baking sheet with ungreased parchment paper and scoop 2 tablespoons of the mixture onto the baking sheet. Repeat until the mixture is used up, dropping several inches apart. Bake at 350° for 4 to 6 minutes, or until golden brown. While the cookies are still warm, shape over the bottom of a small ramekin or cup until cool. Gently remove from the ramekin. To serve, place a cookie basket upright on a plate. Scoop one of each of the sorbets into the basket and place a few tablespoons of the reserved raspberry purée at the base of the basket on one side. Sprinkle with raspberries and dust with powdered sugar.

Makes 4 servings

— *THE INN AT MONTCHANIN VILLAGE*

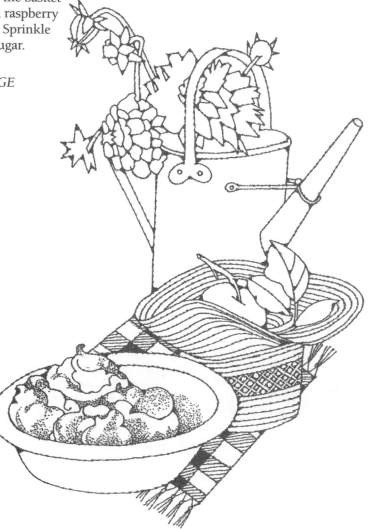

Mocha Chocolate Filbert Pâté with White Chocolate Sauce

Featuring one of Oregon's most notable natural products, the hazelnut or filbert, this delicious dessert may just be the answer to your wildest chocolate fantasy. Begin preparing this recipe several hours before serving, or the day before.

SAUCE
- 8 ounces quality white chocolate
- 1 cup heavy cream
- ¼ cup brandy, rum, or nutty liqueur of choice

PÂTÉ
- ¼ cup water
- 2 drops canola oil
- 12 ounces semisweet chocolate
- 2 tablespoons butter

- 2 tablespoons brewed strong coffee
- 3 tablespoons hazelnut liqueur
- 1 tablespoon vanilla extract
- 3 egg yolks
- ½ cup whipping cream
- 2 tablespoons sugar
- ¼ cup coarsely chopped filberts

GARNISHES
- Raspberries
- Fresh mint leaves

Begin by preparing the sauce. Thinly shave the chocolate or process until finely ground.

Heat the cream and liqueur in a small saucepan over medium-high heat. Cook until the cream starts to thicken. Remove from the heat and add the shaved or ground chocolate, stirring until it is well combined. Set aside and prepare the pâté. (Note that the sauce may be made ahead of time and stored in the refrigerator as the liqueur acts as a preservative.)

To begin the pâté, mix the water and the oil and lightly brush a loaf pan 4 x 6 inches.

In the top of a double boiler, melt the chocolate, butter, and coffee over simmering water. When melted, remove from the heat and add the liqueur and vanilla. Beat in the egg yolks, one at a time, making sure that the first is incorporated before adding the next. Cool to room temperature.

Whip the cream with the sugar until soft peaks form.

Stir half of the whipped cream into the chocolate mixture. Gently fold in the remaining cream and the filberts. Place in the loaf pan and refrigerate for 2 to 3 hours, or until set. Slice and serve with a pool of sauce spooned first onto the bottom of the serving plate. Garnish with fresh berries and mint leaves.

Makes 8 to 10 servings

— *THE STEAMBOAT INN*

Tortilla Flower Saucers

Quick to make, these simple flower saucers made by cutting and deep-frying tortillas, make a very easy but impressive dessert in the shape of a saucer or bowl, depending on how well the ladle coaxes the shape. We have suggested a filling here for the saucers, but you may concoct any desired combination.

8 flour tortillas, 6-inch size
  Oil for deep frying
2 tablespoons sugar
½ teaspoon ground cinnamon
1 quart ice cream or yogurt of choice

2 cups fresh berries or mixed fresh fruits
¾ cup chopped nuts
¾ cup or more caramel sauce or sweet sauce of choice

Cut the tortillas into flower shapes with kitchen shears by snipping petals in a circular pattern. Petals should be about 1 to 1½ inches at the base. Be sure to leave enough of a flower center, about 2½ inches, to hold a couple of scoops of ice cream. Discard tortilla scraps, saving a few as testers.

In a large heavy saucepan, heat 2 inches of oil until very hot. Test by dropping one of the tortilla scraps into the pan. Oil is ready when tortillas immediately sizzle. Cook the tortillas, one at a time. using a ladle to hold the tortilla down in the center, forming a saucer or bowl shape. Remove tortillas with tongs and drain oil on paper towel.

Sift together the sugar and cinnamon and sprinkle over the tortillas while they are still warm. Fill the bowls or saucers with ice cream, fruit, nuts, and sauce, and serve immediately.

Makes 8 servings

— *APACHE CANYON RANCH*

ALWAYS OF SERVICE

Pantry Staples

Old-Time Soup Crackers

Chef Joan Dawkins remembers making these crackers with her grandfather when she was growing up in the early 1930s. Once you have tested them, you will think twice about buying crackers prepackaged.

1½ cups all-purpose flour
1 teaspoon salt
½ teaspoon cayenne pepper
½ cup (1 stick) unsalted butter, cut into pieces
1½ cups Parmesan cheese, grated

2 large egg yolks, mixed with 2 tablespoons cold water
Sesame, rye, or celery seeds, as desired for topping the crackers

In the bowl of a food processor, combine the flour, salt, and cayenne pepper. Add the butter all at once and process until the mixture resembles coarse meal. Add the cheese and then the egg mixture as the machine is running. Process a few times just to form a dough, (do not overmix). Gather into a flattened ball, cover with plastic wrap, and chill for 1 hour.

Preheat the oven to 350°. Divide the dough in half. Roll 1 of the halves into a rectangle ¼-inch thick. Fold into thirds and rotate a quarter of a turn. Roll, fold, and rotate 2 more times, finishing with the dough folded into thirds. Repeat the procedure with a second piece of dough.

Roll the dough out to ⅛-inch thick. Cut into decorative shapes. Prick each cracker several times with a fork. Garnish with sesame seeds or garnish of choice. Place crackers onto ungreased baking sheets and bake for 20 minutes, turning each cracker over after 10 minutes. Remove from the oven when golden and cool in baking pans over wire racks.

Makes 40 crackers

— *ORCHARD HILL COUNTRY INN*

Artichoke Dip

Although delicious as a dip with crudités, chips, or crackers, the folks at Bear Creek Lodge like this recipe best with a bit of tapenade and goat cheese on thin slices of freshly baked French bread.

1 can (14 ounces) artichoke hearts in water
¼ cup mayonnaise
¾ cup freshly grated Parmesan cheese

3 ounces cream cheese
2 teaspoons minced fresh dill
1 clove garlic, minced
Fresh black pepper to taste

Preheat the oven to 350°. Place all of the ingredients into a food processor and pulse to a fine chop, just before the mixture would turn into a purée. Place the dip into a small ovenproof bowl and bake for 30 minutes, or until just lightly golden on top.

Makes 2 cups

— *BEAR CREEK LODGE*

Oriental Peanut Dip

The spicy flavors in this unusual dip contrast magnificently with fresh vegetables such as cucumbers, carrots, and broccoli florets. The inn has many picnic recipes, sending them with its guests out to hiking trails and intimate streams.

½ cup unsalted fresh peanut butter
2 green onions, minced
6 cloves garlic, minced
⅓ cup low-salt, natural soy sauce
1 teaspoon minced fresh ginger

2 to 3 teaspoons hot chili oil
2 tablespoons honey
¼ cup sweet-rice wine
2 tablespoons minced fresh cilantro

Combine all of the above ingredients, mixing well. Cover and refrigerate until ready to take out on the picnic or serve with crackers and crudités at cocktail hour.

Makes 1 to 1½ cups

— *THE STEAMBOAT INN*

Molasses–Apple Cider Glaze

Although this is meant for the Fire-Roasted Salmon with Molasses–Apple Cider Glaze on page 89, you may use this as a barbecue sauce for other seafood, pork, and chicken.

1 cup molasses   ¼ cup apple cider or juice
⅛ cup soy sauce

Combine all of the above ingredients.
    Makes 1½ cups glaze

    — *THE CAPTAIN WHIDBEY INN*

Dill-Dijon Salad Dressing

The teaming of these strong ingredients makes a powerful accompaniment to fresh baby field greens. It is delightful for a lunch or dinner salad.

¼ cup Dijon-style mustard   1 tablespoon chopped fresh dill
¼ cup mayonnaise   leaves
3 tablespoons (¼ cup)   2 tablespoons honey
    sour cream   1 tablespoon cider vinegar
3 tablespoons buttermilk   Salt and white pepper to taste

Combine all of the ingredients and whisk well. Serve ladled over a salad.
    Makes 1 cup

    — *GLACIER BAY COUNTRY INN*

Herbed Focaccia Bread

Enjoy this traditional Italian flatbread baked with a variety of toppings such as they do at the inn: caramelized onions, roasted garlic with grated cheese, tomatoes and roasted peppers. Focaccia also makes a nice base for a pizza topped with your tummy's desire.

¼ cup warm water
2 tablespoons olive oil
1 tablespoon active dry yeast
3 cups unbleached all-purpose flour
1 teaspoon salt
½ teaspoon ground black pepper
¾ cup water

¼ cup chopped fresh herbs such as basil, oregano, rosemary, sage (whatever complements the toppings or meal you are serving)
Cornmeal for baking pan
Olive oil spray

In a large bowl, combine the ¼ cup warm water with the olive oil and then sprinkle in the yeast, stirring to combine. Let the mixture sit until it begins to proof, or bubble. Combine the flour, salt, and pepper, then add to the yeast mixture with remaining ¾ cup water. Stir to blend, then turn out onto a floured surface and knead until smooth and shiny, about 4 minutes. Add the herbs and continue to knead for another 4 minutes. Transfer the dough to an oiled bowl, turning to coat all sides; cover with plastic wrap and a towel and let rise until doubled in bulk, about 1 hour.

Gently punch the dough down; replace covers and let rise again for another 30 minutes. Preheat the oven to 450° and place a cooking stone in the oven. Flour a work surface and divide the dough into halves, pulling and stretching each half until each is 12 inches round (or make 6 to 8 individual rounds per half).

Transfer the dough to a baking sheet or bread peel that has been sprinkled with cornmeal. Cover with plastic for 20 minutes, then gently tap the surface with your fingertips so as to lightly dimple the dough. Spray the surface lightly with olive oil. Slide the dough onto the hot stone. Put 4 ice cubes in the bottom of the oven for moisture, and bake for about 15 minutes, or until golden brown.

Makes 2 loaves

— BEAR CREEK LODGE

Cornbread

This recipe yields enough cornbread for the Sausage, Apple, and Cheese Curried-Cornbread Pudding on pages 10–11.

1 tablespoon shortening
1 cup yellow cornmeal
½ cup whole-wheat flour
2 teaspoons baking powder
1 teaspoon salt

1 cup skim milk
1 egg
1 tablespoon canola oil
3 tablespoons honey

Melt the shortening in a 9-inch-square baking pan or cast-iron skillet, while preheating the oven to 375°.

In a medium mixing bowl, combine the cornmeal, whole-wheat flour, baking powder, and salt. Mix well; set aside.

In another medium bowl, whisk together the milk, egg, oil, and honey. Add this wet mixture to the cornmeal-flour mixture and stir well. The batter will be very runny.

Remove the pan from the oven and carefully swirl the pan to coat with the shortening. Pour in the batter and return the pan to the oven. Bake for 25 minutes, or until golden brown. Let cool and remove from the pan.

Makes 8 to 10 servings

— *THE INN AT 410*

Homemade Crusty French Bread

Elizabeth Turney, innkeeper and chef, waxes poetic as she offers this intro-duction to her bread: "While this bread does not require huge amounts of your time, it does need time; a good crusty bread is not to be rushed. You need to be in the mood to bake bread. Pick a day when you have the time to soak in a bath as the bread rises or to curl up with a good book or a cup of tea. Homemade bread is affected by the essence of your day. It may be all in your head, but you will notice a difference between a bread made with time and comfort, and one from stress and stolen moments. This recipe will take four hours before you can reap the joys of your labor, but it only requires about forty minutes of your time; the rest is the bread's time! Pull the bread apart while warm, close your eyes, and savor the moment."

¾ cup warm water	2¾ cups unbleached all-purpose
1½ tablespoons active dry yeast	flour
1 teaspoon sugar	Olive oil spray
1½ cups warm water	Cornmeal for pans
1 tablespoon coarse sea salt	Sesame and poppy seeds for
2¾ cups unbleached bread flour	tops of loaves

Pour the ¾ cup of water into a large bread bowl. Sprinkle in the yeast and sugar and stir until blended. Let this sit until foamy, about 10 minutes. Add the remaining water, salt, and bread flour, and mix either by hand or with an electric mixer until blended. Gradually add the all-purpose flour, mixing with a spoon until the mixture forms a ball and pulls away from the sides of the bowl. (Do not despair; you may not use all of the flour.)

Sprinkle flour on a clean work surface and turn the dough out, adding flour as you knead, until the dough is elastic and the surface is smooth. Allow 5 to 10 minutes for kneading; do not rush yourself on your bread. Oil a bowl with olive oil or no-stick cooking oil spray, and place the dough down in it, then turn over so as to oil both sides. Cover with a plastic wrap to contain the moisture and cover again with a towel to retain the warmth. Set the dough in a warm (not hot) place where it can be left to rise undisturbed for 1½ hours. When the dough has doubled in bulk, punch down the center; cover again with plastic and cloth and let sit for another 1½ hours, or until doubled again in size.

Preheat the oven to 425°. Punch the dough again and turn it out onto a floured work surface to shape the loaves (in rectangular French

or baguette shapes or in round free form). Cut the dough into 2 to 3 pieces and shape as desired. Prepare pans by spraying with olive oil, then sprinkle a French loaf pan, or a baking sheet for round loaves, with cornmeal. Put loaves in pan and sprinkle loaves lightly with the poppy seeds, cover with plastic and cloth, and let rise again until doubled in bulk. Diagonally slice the top of the dough 3 to 4 times with a sharp knife. Mist the loaves with water and place in the oven for 35 to 40 minutes if you make 2 loaves and 25 to 30 minutes for 3 baguettes. Mist again after 10 minutes, acting quickly so as not to lose oven heat. (You may also add 4 to 5 ice cubes to the oven to add steam. The more moisture, the crunchier the crust.) Bread is done when golden and the crust sounds hollow when tapped. Let the bread sit for a few minutes to cool to warm; then place on the table to be pulled apart.

Makes 2 loaves or 3 baguettes

— *BEAR CREEK LODGE*

Roasted Garlic

1 head garlic   ½ cup water
2 tablespoons olive oil

Preheat the oven to 375°. Remove the top of the garlic bulb. Rub the bulb with 1 tablespoon of the oil and place in a small bread pan. Place the water and the remaining oil in the pan. Cover with aluminum foil. Bake in the oven for 1 to 1½ hours, or until the garlic is soft and easily slips out of the skin. Cool. Cover and refrigerate until ready to use.

— *GAIL'S KITCHEN*

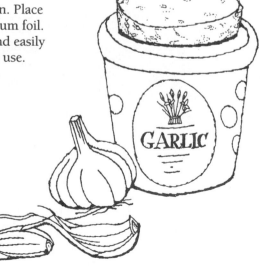

Celeriac Chips

Celeriac is a knobby root of a special celery grown expressly for the root. The vegetable tastes like celery and may be eaten raw or cooked. You can also grate the root over a salad or make celeriac slaw by cutting the root into julienne and then adding coleslaw flavorings. Here, thin disks of the root are deep-fried and sprinkled with seasoning. Celeriac chips are curious-looking garnishes, but they always draw rave reviews for their clean taste and flowerlike appearance when puffed up after frying.

4 cups frying oil   Salt and pepper
1 large celery root bulb

Heat the oil in a wok to about 300°. Clean the celery root and slice it into paper-thin chips. Fry in the hot oil until golden brown. Drain on a paper towel and season with salt and pepper.
   — *SAN SOPHIA INN*

Homemade Pasta

The pasta may be made up to 2 days in advance of serving time. If making it the same day, you will need an hour for the pasta to chill before shaping and an hour for drying finished pasta shapes before cooking.

1 cup semolina pasta flour   1 cup warm water
1 tablespoon coarse salt
2 tablespoons extra-virgin olive
   oil

Place the flour and salt into a large mixing bowl such as a pasta serving bowl. Mixing with a fork, add the olive oil and water gradually to form a soft dough. Turn the dough out onto a clean work surface and knead for 10 minutes, or until the dough is soft and smooth. Wrap the dough in plastic and refrigerate for 1 hour or up to 2 days.

MAKING THE SHAPES:
   Orecchiette, or little ears: Cut the dough into 8 even pieces. Make ropes out of the dough about ½ inch in diameter by rolling dough onto a clean work surface. Cut each rope into ¼-inch disks. With your

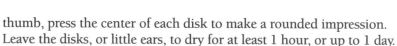

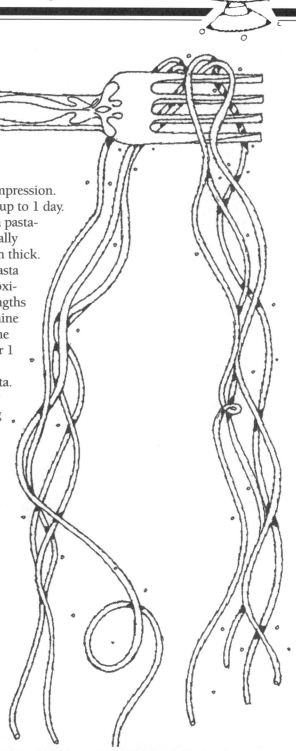

thumb, press the center of each disk to make a rounded impression. Leave the disks, or little ears, to dry for at least 1 hour, or up to 1 day.

Linguine: Divide the dough into 4 equal parts. Using a pasta-rolling machine, put the dough through the rollers, gradually decreasing the thickness until the sheet of dough is ⅛-inch thick. Repeat with the remaining 3 pieces of dough. Allow the pasta sheets to dry for 5 minutes; then cut each sheet into approximately 12-inch lengths. You should have three 12-inch lengths for each sheet. Use the linguine cutter on the rolling machine and cut each sheet into ¼-inch-wide strands. Hang linguine on a drying rack or use the back of a kitchen chair. Dry for 1 hour or longer.

When your sauce is ready, begin cooking the fresh pasta. Cook 1 pound of pasta in at least 5 quarts of boiling water until *al dente,* or having enough body to bite but not being soft or mushy. For pasta that has been drying for about 1 hour, you need only 2 to 4 minutes to cook it. The best way to tell pasta cooking time is to test it every minute or so as it cooks.

Makes 1 pound of pasta

— *THE CAPTAIN FREEMAN INN*

139

Almond Bread Birds

Birds of dough were not an uncommon delicacy on the tables of knights and lords of the castle. Thus, they also make their way onto the table at Ravenwood Castle. These are fun for almost any meal from breakfast to parties.

½ cup slivered toasted almonds
½ cup (1 stick) butter, melted
1 cup very hot water
⅓ cup sugar
2 tablespoons molasses
1 egg

1 tablespoon yeast
1 cup whole-wheat flour
2 cups all-purpose flour
　Currants or raisins for bird
　eyes

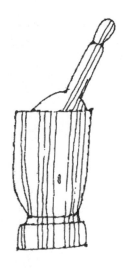

Crush the toasted almonds and set aside. In a large bowl, mix by hand the butter, water, sugar, salt, molasses, and the egg, blending to incorporate. Add the yeast and let sit for 5 minutes to activate. Add the crushed nuts and both the flours, mixing to incorporate. Add more all-purpose flour, if necessary, to make a workable dough. Knead lightly for about 5 minutes. Let the dough rise for about 1 hour.

To form the birds, begin with one quarter of the dough. Form 8 balls of about equal size to make the heads for the birds; set aside. Using the remainder of the dough, shape 8 larger-size balls that will form the body of the birds. Elongate the larger balls into oval shapes for the bodies. Pull one of the ends into a tail. Set a small ball on the other end for the head, using a few drops of water to help the dough adhere as you press the head in place. Make a beak with 2 almond slivers and press currants or raisins into the dough for eyes.

Let the dough rise again in a warm place for another 30 minutes. Place on a baking sheet and bake in a 375° oven for 15 to 18 minutes, or until lightly browned. Serve in a basket presented to the table.

Makes 8 breads

— *RAVENWOOD CASTLE*

Cranberry Relish

Although this recipe accompanies the Turkey Croissant Sandwiches on page 60, I have added it to the pantry section because it is great to have on hand for serving with crackers or with pork and poultry dishes, too.

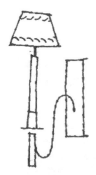

¾ cup water
1½ cups whole cranberries, fresh or frozen

¾ cup sugar
1 teaspoon grated orange rind
¼ cup fresh orange juice

Combine the above ingredients in a nonreactive saucepan over medium heat. Simmer until the liquid is absorbed and the ingredients reach a relish consistency, about 20 to 30 minutes. Remove the mixture from the heat. If using immediately, keep warm; otherwise, cool to room temperature and refrigerate in an airtight container. This stores well for several weeks in the refrigerator.

Makes 1¼ cups

— *THE STEAMBOAT INN*

Black Bean Salsa

Delicious as a condiment for a number of dishes, including poultry and seafood, or as a dip with taco chips. The inn serves the salsa with it's Charleston Shrimp 'n' Grits recipe on pages 22–23. Innkeeper Patty Show says to prepare the salsa a day ahead of time so that the flavors blend. Store in the refrigerator.

1 large tomato, cut into ½-inch dice
1 green bell pepper, cut into ½-inch dice
1 yellow bell pepper, cut into ½-inch dice
½ small red onion, finely diced
¾ cup cooked black beans

2 tablespoons balsamic vinegar
¼ cup tomato juice
1 tablespoon sugar
1 teaspoon salt
½ teaspoon black pepper
2 cloves garlic, minced
3 to 5 drops hot sauce

Mix all of the above ingredients in a large mixing bowl and serve.

Makes 8 servings

— *THE ASHLEY INN*

Italian Eggplant Salsa

Besides servings as a tasty aside to the Breakfast Calzone on page 13, this recipe can also be used as a sauce over pasta or grilled chicken breasts. Innkeeper Kate Nieman, who created this recipe, also serves the salsa in baked phyllo cups (in frozen section of store), sprinkled with toasted pine nuts and baked in a 350° oven for 10 minutes.

10 green onions, tops included
 2 cloves garlic
 2 medium eggplants, peeled
 2 red bell peppers, seeded and coarsely chopped
 2 cans (28 ounces each) Roma tomatoes
½ cup dry red wine
 4 tablespoons Italian seasoning
 1 pound quality country bacon, cooked and broken into small pieces

¾ cup grated Romano cheese
Seasoned pepper or freshly ground black pepper to taste

GARNISH
 Fresh basil
 Toasted pine nuts (optional)

In a food processor, chop the green onions and the garlic for a few seconds; set aside. Peel and coarsely chop the eggplant in the processor with the red peppers.

Place the vegetables into a Dutch oven. Drain the liquid from the cans of tomatoes into the pot; chop the tomatoes and add to the pot. Add the wine and the Italian seasoning. Stir well and cook over medium-low heat for 20 minutes or until juices are thickened; do not let the salsa get too soupy. Add the bacon and the cheese and cover the pot. Reduce the heat to low and simmer for another 10 minutes. Season to taste. Stir in chopped basil and some pine nuts, if desired. Refrigerate or serve immediately.

Makes 2 quarts

— *WASHINGTON HOUSE INN*

Miniature Apple Dumplings

These morsels of pastry and warm apples are a cinch to make and may be served during breakfast, as a snack, for tea-time, or even as a tasty bite on the dinner table with such entrées as pork or chicken. Elmo's grandmother would have these, piping hot with a glass of milk, waiting for him when he came home from school to enjoy while he listened to The Lone Ranger and Tom Mix *on the radio!*

1 can flaky biscuits (8 to a can)
  Nutmeg to taste
½ cup (1 stick) butter, melted
3 cans (14 ounces each) fried
  apples or apple pie filling (or
  cut-up peeled, fresh apples,
  sprinkled with sugar and set
  overnight to develop a syrup)

¼ cup raisins
  Cinnamon to taste
2 egg whites

Separate the layers of the biscuits; you should have 30 to 40. Using a small muffin tin, push a biscuit layer down into each cup, forming a pocket. Add nutmeg and ¼ teaspoon of the melted butter. Add an apple or 2, and 3 or 4 raisins. Sprinkle with cinnamon. Make sure you leave enough dough at the top to mash together and seal.
Seal the dough over the filling and brush with egg white. Remove the dumpling from the muffin pan and place on a greased baking sheet, top side up. Bake at 350° for 25 to 30 minutes, or until the tops are brown.

Makes 30 to 40 dumplings

— *COUSINS B & B*

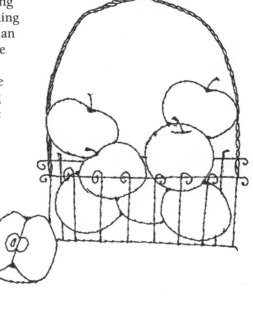

Miss Scarlett's Sorbet

Remember what happened to me when I tasted this delicious sorbet during a television episode featuring The Cedars Plantation! Oh, how I danced the afternoon away à la Tara and the times of Scarlett O'Hara. Serve this to your friends and who knows what they may dream about. The inn uses muscadine wine produced by the Old South Winery in Natchez. Any muscadine or berry wine will do nicely.

2 cups water
1 cup sugar
1½ cups muscadine wine

GARNISH
Fresh cherries or berries
Mint sprigs

Make a simple syrup of water and sugar, boiling the ingredients in a medium saucepan over medium-high heat. Remove from the heat when the sugar dissolves. Stir in the wine. Let cool and then pour into a freezer container. Freeze. Serve with a melon scoop. Garnish with a cherry and mint or a berry and mint.

Makes about 1 pint

— THE CEDARS PLANTATION

Flower-Scented Sugar

Flower- and herb-scented sugars may be used in any recipe calling for sugar; a pleasant addition to cakes, custards, and cookies. If the recipe calls for sugar, think flavored sugar, suggests innkeeper Donna Stone.

1 clear pint-sized jar with tight-fitting lid
White sugar
Petals of edible flowers such as rose, lilac, violets, or any other aromatic flower

1 vanilla bean

Fill the jar one quarter full with sugar. Add a small handful of flowers over the sugar to cover. Add more flowers until you are within ½ inch of the top. Secure the lid and place on a shelf in a cool, dark place. Let the sugar sit for 3 to 4 weeks before using. The longer it sits, the more flavorful it becomes.

— THE WILDFLOWER INN

Rose Flower Jelly

*Enjoyable on nearly any piece of toast, this is especially delicious with the
Rose Petal Muffins made with rose petals on page 40.*

3½ cups edible rose petals
 2 cups water
½ cup sugar
 1 cup white grape juice

1 package powdered fruit
pectin
3 cups white sugar

Bring all but ½ cup of the rose petals, the water, and the sugar to a boil
in a medium saucepan. Reduce the heat to simmer and cook for 5
minutes longer, stirring occasionally. Remove the pan from the heat
Let stand, covered, for several hours or overnight. Strain the syrup,
discarding the flower petals.

Combine the syrup with the grape juice and the pectin in a small
saucepan, mixing well. Bring the mixture to a boil and boil for 1
minute, stirring occasionally. Add the remaining 3 cups of sugar; mix
well. Bring to a full rolling boil that will not stir down. Boil for 1
minute. Remove from the heat. Place the remaining ¼ cup rose petals
in a hot sterilized 1-cup jar. Ladle the jelly into jars, leaving a ½-inch
space at the top; seal with 2-piece lids. Drape the jars with a towel.
Cool to room temperature and store in a cool place.

Makes 4 cups

— *THE WILDFLOWER INN*

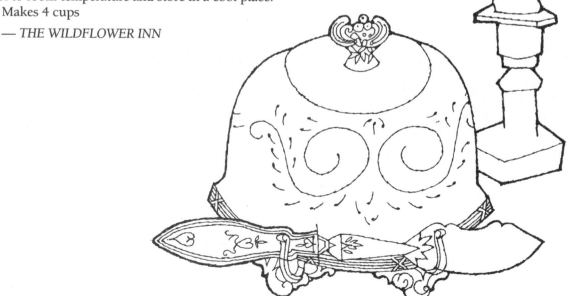

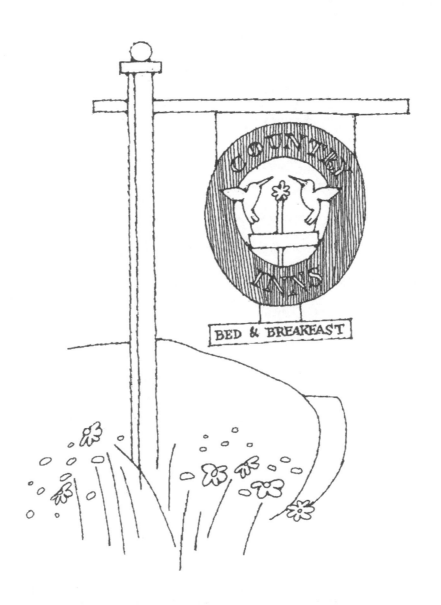

INN DIRECTORY

APACHE CANYON RANCH

4 Canyon Drive
Canoncito, NM 87026
(505) 836-7220
Innkeeper/Owners: Ava Marie
and Theron Bowers
Rooms: 5

Elegance in the midst of ancient mesas . . . this small B&B sits surrounded by many Native American reservations. The influence of cultures comes together here at this African-American-owned inn where hospitality and friendship are commonplace. Ava Marie and Theron built the adobe-style building, just thirty miles outside of Albuquerque.

THE ASHLEY INN

201 Ashley Avenue
Charleston, SC 29403
(803) 723-1848
Innkeeper: Patty Show. Owners:
Bud and Sally Allen
Rooms: 7

The romantic city of Charleston lists many places to stay, but this one is at the top of the list with delicious, thoughtful breakfasts. Bud and Sally also have another elegant property, the Cannonboro, which they also restored. Patty is a professional cook, and guests don't know what to admire first, the gardens, the rooms, or the cooking.

BEAR CREEK LODGE

1184 Bear Creek Trail
Victor, MT 59875
(406) 642-3750
Innkeeper/Owners: Roland and
Elizabeth Turney
Rooms: 8

The Bitterroot is a lovely flower that blooms pink in spring, but it is also the name given to one of the most beautiful areas in America. And this is home to Bear Creek Lodge, one of the country's finest inns. Logs built from a Yellowstone fire warm the lodge but the personalities of the innkeepers even more so. Nature alone gives you reason to visit this relaxed place. The cooking gives you another.

147

BLUE HILL INN

Union Street
Blue Hill, ME 04614
(207) 374-2844
Innkeeper/Owners: Mary and
 Don Hartley
Rooms: 12

When you think of country inns, you think of classic New England, personal service with the owners present in an intimate setting, exciting things going on, and of course, great food. Blue Hill Inn is just that kind of place.

THE CAPTAIN FREEMAN INN

15 Breakwater Road
Brewster, Cape Cod, MA 02631
(508) 896-7481
Innkeeper/Owners: Tom and
 Carol Edmondson
Rooms: 12

In the late 1860s, Captain William Freeman built this mansion in the charming Cape Cod village of Brewster. At the time, the city was home to more deep-water captains than anywhere else in America. Breakfast is the main meal served here, but Carol holds cooking classes throughout the year when dinner is part of the package deal. In winter, you also get to see Tom's extensive orchid-growing hobby.

THE CAPTAIN WHIDBEY INN

2072 W. Captain Whidbey Inn
 Road
Coupeville, WA 98239
(360) 678-4097
Owner: John Colby Stone
Rooms: 32

This romantic, rustic log inn that dates to the early 1900s gives you a peaceful rest with Northwest coastal cuisine and fine wines. Spot eagles or herons, and sail Penn Cove on a day cruise.

THE CEDARS PLANTATION

Route 553
Church Hill, MS 39120
(601) 445-2203
Innkeeper/Owner: Glenda
    Robinson
Rooms: 4

Formerly a plantation, this inn has all of the tradition of the old South in modern times. During the good weather seasons, the gardens are reason enough to visit. The food is homey and hearty with a touch of southern elegance.

COUSINS B&B

303 Turner Street
Beaufort, NC 28516
(919) 504-3478
In|nkeeper/Owners: Elmo and
Martha Barnes
Rooms: 4

Elmo Barnes is the Justin Wilson of bed and breakfasts with his down-home southern/Creole and Bayou-style cooking. Beaufort is a small fishing village, away from the madding crowds.

THE DAVY JACKSON INN

85 Perry Avenue
Jackson Hole, WY 83001
(307) 739-2294
Innkeeper/Owners: Kay and
    Gordon Minns
Rooms: 11

Visiting Jackson Hole's quaint western village with very nice shopping is topped off by returning to the casual but well-appointed Davy Jackson Inn. Rooms are complete with whirlpool tubs and easy decorating by Kay. Beds are sumptuous, and you have a great night's sleep here. Some of the rooms have fainting couches. After a day of outdoor activities from snowmobiling to dogsledding and nature-watching, one is ready to slink back into one of these casual sofas—a way that the inn enjoys pampering its guests.

GLACIER BAY COUNTRY INN

P.O. Box 5
Gustavus, AK 99826
(907) 697-2288
Innkeeper/Owners Sandi and Ken
    Marchbanks
Rooms: 21

The inn is a large, rambling, rustic, and homey lodge near Glacier Bay National Park. Even though out in the middle of nowhere, this perfectly warm and inviting place serves fabulous cuisine by a professional chef.

GLORIA'S SPOUTING HORN B&B

4464 Lawai Beach Road
Poipu Beach, Kauai, HI 96756
(808) 742-6995
Innkeeper/Owners: Bob and
    Gloria Merkle
Rooms: 3 suites

Rooms have views that are worth a million dollars. Gloria's has been around for many years and even weathered a recent devastating hurricane. Bob and Gloria had five rooms then but decided to make two fewer but much larger. Gloria's has never disappointed me. The true essence of a Hawaiian vacation can be found here.

THE INN AT 410

410 North Leroux
Flagstaff, AZ 86001
(520) 774-0088
Innkeeper/Owners: Howard and
    Sally Krueger
Rooms: 8

Tucked into a charming old residential neighborhood, the inn is a few blocks from downtown Flagstaff, a tall pine-tree-scalloped village that blends the old with the new. Native American ruins are only minutes away, and the Grand Canyon is an hour-and-half drive. Breakfast at the Inn at 410 is always healthy and tasty. Innkeeper Sally Krueger is a creative chef. Come back for afternoon tea and you will find the emphasis is more on having a good time with some delicious snacks.

THE INN AT MAPLEWOOD FARM

447 Center Road
Hillsborough, NH 03244
(603) 464-4242
Innkeeper/Owners: Laura and
 Jaymes Simoes
Rooms: 5

Drive up to the white-clapboard farmhouse with the black shutters, and the innkeepers greet you with a broad smile and a warm welcome. Rooms are simply but admirably furnished with spacious baths. In the morning, cowbells jingle next door, and an award-winning breakfast is ready for you to indulge. Old-time radios from the innkeeper Jayme Simoes's collection offer an evening turndown as the voices from *The Shadow* to *Fibber Magee and Molly* play on as long as you wish. This is a special little bed and breakfast not to be missed.

THE INN AT MONTCHANIN VILLAGE

Route 100 and Kirk Road
Wilmington, DE 19710
(302) 888-2133
Owners: Missy and Dan Lickle
Rooms: 22

There is so much to do and see in the Brandywine area — from Longwood Gardens to the famed Winterthur Museum, that you want to stay out and explore all day. But the charming style of this tiny hamlet with its gas lamps and brick walkways, leads you to such luxurious and comfortable guests suites that you are just as excited to get back as to go out for an adventure. The inn is a cluster of buildings that housed DuPont employees who worked at nearby gunpowder mills. The food at the inn's Krazy Kats restaurant is top-notch.

INN AT OLDE NEW BERLIN

321 Market Street
New Berlin, PA 17855
(717) 966-0321
Innkeeper/Owners: Nancy and
   John Showers
Rooms: 7

Victorian hospitality abounds at this classic country inn. Dining is at small tables in the 19th-century dining room and front parlor of this turreted little mansion on the main street through town. Antiques fill comfortable rooms and full breakfasts make mornings worth waking for.

INN AT LE ROSIER

314 E. Main Street
New Iberia, LA 70560
(318) 367-5306
Innkeeper/Owner: Hallman
   Woods Jr.
Rooms: 4

The mist hangs heavy over the bayous in early morning and nothing could be more peaceful or beautiful for that moment, except, of course, the inn itself. Le Rozier is first a great place to dine in elegant settings and second, to rest for the night in rooms that make you feel special.

INN AT VAUCLUSE SPRING

140 Vaucluse Spring Lane
Stephens City, VA 22655
(540) 869-0200
Innkeeper/Owners: Karen and
   Mike Caplanis and Neil and
   Barry Myers
Rooms: 12

The inn is a country retreat with restored buildings. A spring runs through it, right under one of the guest cottages! The gentle surrounding farmland and the simple, yet elegant country style of the decor, food, and the innkeepers have put this at the top part of my list of favorites.

ORCHARD HILL COUNTRY INN

2502 Washington Street
Julian, CA 92036
(612) 765-1700
Innkeepers/Owners: Pat and
 Darrell Straube
Rooms: 21

The town of Julian is one of my favorites in the United States. Orchard Hill is nestled into the hillside overlooking the town, which is a quick walk to shops and all the apple pie you could possibly want. Folks come to Julian just to stand in line for a slice of homemade pie at one of the three-block town's three or four apple pie bakeries. The hills are alive with apples growing in season. The inn is every bit as charming, with sophistication and delicious cuisine.

THE PLANTATION INN/GERARD'S RESTAURANT

174 Lahainaluna Road
Lahaina, Maui, HI 96761
(808) 667-9225
Innkeeper: Chuck Robinson
Rooms: 19

Oftentimes, it is the food that makes the inn. Indeed, Chef Gerard Reversade's fine French cuisine, sometimes served with a tropical flair, has given the inn worldwide attention. But the rooms at the inn, all individually decorated with a Casablanca feel, and the incredible warmth of the staff, make this a must place to stay if visiting Lahaina.

RAVENWOOD CASTLE

65666 Bethel Road
New Plymouth, OH 45654
(614) 596-2606
Innkeeper/Owner: Sue Maxwell
Rooms: 8

Everyone thinks of the time when he or she can spend a day as a princess, prince, king, or queen. If you stay at a B&B or country inn where pampering is the first order of the day, you will feel like royalty. At Ravenwood Castle, they take that notion rather literally as you are surrounded by all things noble in this mansion that the owner and her husband built from scratch only a few years ago. The tearoom is as enchanting as the castle itself and just as elegant. Leave your everyday expectations behind and let your imagination fill in the rest at Ravenwood.

SAN SOPHIA INN

330 W. Pacific Avenue
Telluride, CO 81435
(970) 728-3001
Innkeeper/Owners: Keith and
    Alicia Hampton and Andie
    Davison
Rooms: 17

Set back almost against one of Telluride's majestic mountains of the San Juan range, this thoroughly modern Victorian is the place to stay for quiet and for good food. Keith and Alicia are not only good at hospitality but also at choosing the best wines to go with the food of the inn's dynamic young chef.

THE SOUTHERN HOTEL

146 Third Street
Ste. Genevieve, MO 63670
(573) 883-3493
Innkeeper/Owners: Barbara and
   Mike Hankins
Rooms: 7

All of the magic of a small village is here in Ste. Genevieve, where the pace is as slow as the river can be. The Southern Hotel leaves a striking impression on you. It is one of those unforgettable places to stay. Perhaps it's Barbara's great food, Mike's humor, or the gardens that they both revere. Whatever, your life is somehow changed, in some small way, by a visit to the inn and the town.

THE STEAMBOAT INN

42705 North Umpqua Highway
Steamboat, OR 97447
(541) 498-2411
Innkeeper/Owners: Jim and
   Sharon Van Loan
Manager and Chef: Patricia Lee
Rooms: 15

A variety of accommodations sits along the scenic Umpqua River, from cottages to cabins and private suites. Steamboat Inn has several personalities from the ardent angler to the romantic couple, and somehow they all come together in harmony at the dinner table, where some of the finest down-home but elegant cooking can be found in the state. Put on your casual clothing and hike and bike and explore the terrain here by day or visit a winery. The inn will pack you a gourmet picnic lunch.

VICTORIAN TREASURE B&B

115 Prairie Street
Lodi, WI 53555
(608) 592-5199
Innkeeper/Owners: Todd and
  Kimberly Seidl
Rooms: 9

Lodi is a quiet town set off on its own, the perfect spot to get away and while away the time on the sprawling front porch at the inn or take a ferryboat ride or stop by and have some true Wisconsin sweet custard. The Victorian Treasure is everything you would expect a B&B to be. The Seidls are hands-on innkeepers who know that their number one job is to serve their guests. The rooms at the inn, especially the historically inspired suites, are real gems.

THE WILDFLOWER INN

167 Palmer Avenue
Falmouth, MA 02540
(508) 548-9524
Innkeeper/Owners: Donna and
  Phil Stone
Rooms: 5

All of the warmth of home and more is waiting for the weary traveler here. Rooms are named after wildflowers and decorated for luxury and with country taste. Breakfast is fresh and sprinkled with flowers to eat, perhaps one in a muffin and another as a garnish. All good things bloom here, including your mood and spirit.

THE WILLIAM PAGE INN

8 Martin Street
Annapolis, MD 21401
(410) 626-1506
Innkeeper/Owners: Robert
  Zachelli and Greg Page
Rooms: 5

Simple historic friendliness greets guests at the B&B as well as full breakfast trays in their room or in the parlor. The inn is located in the heart of the historic district of this easy-going community on the Chesapeake Bay. Annapolis is a walking city with shops to browse in and galleries galore. William Page provides a comfortable, cheerful environment in which to dock for your visit to America's former capital and today's sailing capital.

WASHINGTON HOUSE INN

W62 N573 Washington Avenue
Cedarburg, WI 53012
(414) 375-3550
Innkeeper: Wendy Porterfield
Chef: Kate Niemar
Rooms: 34

Although a slightly larger facility, the Washington House Inn is a special place. Each room is well-appointed and filled with antiques. Rooms are fresh and inviting and the food, although only breakfast, is memorable and literally award-winning. Cedarburg is chockablock with good shops and trees that make strolling a pleasure.

RESOURCE DIRECTORY

On this season's episodes of our Country Inn Cooking *television show, we visited a wide variety of interesting people and places—in addition to the country inns, the innkeepers and the chefs. Here's a list that may help you get in touch with them as well.*

Food and Kitchenwares

49 WEST COFFEEHOUSE, WINE BAR & GALLERY

49 West Street
Annapolis, MD 21401
410-626-9796

A delightful eaterie for any meal—with rotating art exhibits and good music. Right outside the front door is a spectacular view of the historic Annapolis skyline, highlighted by the 1772 State House dome and St. Anne's Church steeple.

APPLE LANE ORCHARD

Don and Mary Hall
P.O. Box 1004
Julian, CA 92036
760-765-2645

Apple grower, supplying bakeries such as Mom's Pie Shop on Main Street in Julian.

BILL'S BOG

William B. Flagg
1150 Harwich Road
Brewster, MA 02631
508-896-8425

Bill Flagg is preserving a historic method of producing cranberries through a dry-picking technique — here on Cape Cod, where cranberries are king.

BLACK FLY CATERING

7074 Bembe Beach Road
Annapolis, MD 21403
410-268-4661

Provider of gourmet foods for all manner of events on land and on water—in the boating community of Annapolis.

CITY DOCK CAFE

18 Market Space
Annapolis, MD 21401
410-269-0969

A favorite spot—near the water and right in the historic district of Annapolis—for great morning coffee and bagels as well as huge lunchtime sandwiches.

THE COOKING COMPANY

Cindy Farny and Monika Callard
Box 1044
Telluride, CO 81435
970-728-3142

Creators of crusty bread loaves, including decorative and unusual breads. They will ship orders around the country.

HANCOCK COUNTY ORGANIC GROWERS

P.O. Box 1293
Blue Hill, ME 04614
207-374-5905

A co-op bringing together the produce of eight farms in the Blue Hill, Maine, area.

HENRY ESTATE WINERY

Scott Henry & Family
P.O. Box 26
Umpqua, OR 97486
541-459-5120

A charming, small, family operation. Scott Henry invented a trellis system that is revolutionizing the way many vineyards grow their grapes.

HOMEPLACE EVERLASTINGS

Debi and Jack Parkin
20518 Beaver Creek Road
Hagerstown, MD 21740
301-791-2756

Debi and Jack Parkin work very hard but live the life many dream of: earning their living from an old stone farmhouse and barn— selling dried flower arrangements from the plants they grow in summer and wonderful gift items all year.

HORSEPOWER FARM

Paul and Mollie Birdstall
Route 15
Penobscot, ME 04614
207-374-5038

Paul and Mollie Birdsall tend to an old-fashioned farm, planting and harvesting with horsepower as the farm's name implies. Other farm animals romp about, including hens that lay fresh eggs supplied to the Blue Hill Inn.

JONES DAIRY FARM

P.O. Box 808
Fort Atkinson, WI 53538
414-563-2431

A long-time, family-owned business supplying supermarkets and specialty stores with high-quality sausage, bacon, and ham. Jones Dairy Farm is an underwriter of *Country Inn Cooking with Gail Greco*.

JULIAN DRUG STORE & SODA FOUNTAIN

Larry and Joan Arico
2134 Main Street
Julian, CA 92036
760-765-0332

A charming, old-fashioned drug store, operated by the owner and a crew of soda jerks who make your mouth water and feel a whole lot better with soda fountain nostalgia and up-to-date fountain delights.

KING ARTHUR FLOUR

Box 1010
Norwich, VT 05055
802-649-3881

One of the country's few producers of organic flour, King Arthur Flour was started by an entrepreneurial couple. Call the company for its fine catalog of baking goods.

MAX BURTON HEALTHY COOKWARE

2322 Holgate Street
Tacoma, WA 98402
800-272-8603
206-627-2665

Makers of fine kitchen stove-top and other handy baking appliances, including the portable butane burners we use on the television show. These portable burners also make a high-quality stove for camping and picnicking.

MOM'S PIE SHOP

Anita Nichols
2119 Main Street
Julian, CA 92036
760-765-2472

Take a step back in time at this fine café, which serves mainly apple pies by the slice and boxes and boxes of pies to take home.

THE MOON CAFE

137 Prince George Street
Annapolis, MD 21401
410-280-1956

The perfect place to relax and contemplate the adventures of a day spent enjoying the sights of the historic district of Annapolis.

NORRIS BLUEBERRY FARM

Paul and Sandy Norris
8181 Oak Hill Road
Roseburg, OR 97470

Paul and Sandy Norris are top-notch blueberry growers, who also provide a truly hands-on employment experience for local teenagers each summer at their farm.

PAIN DE FAMILLE

Cornfield Hill Road
South Brookesville, ME 04617
207-326-9160

Using a wood-fired brick oven, Pain de Famille (or "family bread") bakers produce naturally leavened (sourdough) loaves mixed and formed completely by hand of organic grains, filtered water, unrefined French pearl gray sea salt.

PENN COVE SHELLFISH

Ian and Rawle Jefferds
P.O. Box 148
Coupeville, WA 98239
360-678-4803

North America's largest mussel farm is found just a short boat ride from the Captain Whidbey Inn on Whidbey Island near Seattle.

PEP'S PACKING

Laura "Pep" Coby
P.O. Box 23
Gustavus, AK 99826
907-697-2295

This delightful young woman—known by locals and regulars as Pep—has a well-deserved reputation as the best fish packer in the Glacier Bay, Alaska, area. Guests of the Glacier Bay Country Inn can have their catch packed by Pep for shipment home.

REGAL WARE

1675 Reigle Drive
Kewaskum, WI 53040
414-626-2121

Makers of fine kitchen essentials, including high-quality, nonstick pans in a range of prices, and one of the highest-rated bread-baking machines available. Regal is an underwriter of *Country Inn Cooking with Gail Greco*.

SATUCKET FARM STAND

Route 124
Brewster, MA 02631

The stand where Captain Freeman Inn chef Carol Edmondson shops for fresh ingredients for her fine recipes.

SHARTNER FARMS

Rit Shartner
West Side Road
North Conway, NH 03860

Rit Shartner's mom provided the old-time recipe for making sweet jam from the acres and acres of strawberries Rit grows here.

THE SPICE HOUSE

1031 Old World Third
Milwaukee, WI 53202
414-272-0977

Old-time curiosity shop filled with spices ground to order.

STONYFIELD FARM

Ten Burton Drive
Londonderry, NH 03053
603-437-4040

Stonyfield Farm is a pioneer maker of organic yogurt.

SWEET THINGS

Christine Adams
1200 Gregory Lane
Building 3—#4
Jackson, WY 83001
307-734-0125
307-733-8376

High-quality, handmade chocolates—specialty items for all occasions.

TRYNN GALLERY

Bill Chappelow
27540 Old Highway 80
Guatay, CA 91931
619-473-9030

Maker of highly artistic hand-cut and hand-turned wooden kitchen utensils.

WALNUT ACRES ORGANIC FARMS

Penns Creek, PA 17862
800-433-3998

A classic, mail-order company, this organic-only supplier is family-run—carrying products from granola to homemade soups.

WHITE MOUNTAIN MUSHROOM COMPANY

Dianna Franke
P.O. Box 57
Freedom, NH 03836
603-539-6291

Dianna is the provider of the exotic, delicious mushrooms that are used by chef Laurel Tessier at the Notchland Inn in Hart's Location, New Hampshire. Here is an unusual cottage industry where mushrooms such as king, oyster, and shiitake are grown.

Adventures and Attractions

THE BURNETT FAMILY OF MUSICIANS

6960 Columbine Boulevard
Flagstaff, AZ 86004
520-526-3522

Western and gospel fiddlin' and singin' at its best from the whole family: Ryan, 7; Jessie, 8; Rachel, 11; Lyndsay, 13; and parents: Connie and Brian Burnett. You can hear the Burnetts entertaining at the chuckwagon dinners put on by Hitchin' Post Stables (see listing below) or during an episode of *Country Inn Cooking with Gail Greco.*

BRANDYWINE RIVER MUSEUM

Route 1 and Route 100
Chadds Ford, PA 19317
610-388-2700

Home to the famous Wyeth collections—paintings by three generations: N. C. Wyeth, Andrew, and Jamie.

COUNTRY CARRIAGES

Suzanne Porter and
Wayne Moretti
P.O. Box 607
Julian, CA 92036
760-765-1471

Enjoy a leisurely ride, as we did on the TV show, through the town of Julian and surrounding countryside in a four- or nine-passenger carriage. Evening drives are also available.

COWBOY VILLAGE RESORT AT TOGWOTEE

P.O. Box 91
Highway 26/287
Moran, WY 83013
800-543-2847

The area's premiere snowmobiling resort, with daily tours of Yellowstone National Park.

GEYSER CREEK DOGSLED ADVENTURES

Butch & Norina Shields
P.O. Box 846
Dubois, WY 82513
800-531-MUSH
307-455-2702

Butch and Norina's adventures on dogsleds, and their candlelit gourmet meals at a yurt, deep in the snowy forest, are reason enough to visit Jackson Hole.

GRAND CANYON RAILWAY

123 N. San Francisco
Suite 210
Flagstaff, AZ 86001
520-773-1976

Historic turn-of-the-century steam engines take tourists to the Grand Canyon from Memorial Day weekend through September as do vintage 1950s diesel locomotives the remainder of the year, with entertainment at the departure point in Williams, Arizona, and onboard.

GRAND PACIFIC CHARTERS

Ponch and Sandy Marchbanks
c/o Glacier Bay Country Inn
P.O. Box 5
Gustavus, AK 99826
907-697-2288

Glacier Bay Country Inn innkeepers Ponch and Sandi Marchbanks have their own small fleet of charter boats to provide guests with salmon and halibut fishing expeditions as well as sightseeing adventures in Glacier Bay.

HAGLEY MUSEUM

P.O. Box 3630
Wilmington, DE 19807
302-658-2400

A spectacular setting along the picturesque Brandywine River adds to the fascination inspired by a visit to the DuPont family's original estate, gardens, and company mills.

HAMMOND-HARWOOD HOUSE

19 Maryland Avenue
Annapolis, MD 21401
410-269-1714

An outstanding example of
American Colonial architecture
by the renowned William
Buckland, the Hammond-
Harwood House was built
in 1774 and is a National
Historic Landmark.

HITCHIN' POST STABLES

448 Lake Mary Road
Flagstaff, AZ 86001
520-774-1719

Travel by hayride or horseback to
a wonderfully rustic wagon-train
campsite to enjoy cowboy-
country cooking at its very best
in a real chuck-wagon dinner.

LAHAINA DIVERS

Akiyo Murata, manager
143 Dickenson Street
Lahaina, Maui, HI 96761
808-667-7496

Provider of all manner of snor-
keling and diving gear plus orga-
nized adventures for visitors to
see the endless array of colorful
fish that make their home in the
beautifully clear waters off Maui.

LONGWOOD GARDENS

Route 1
Kennett Square, PA 19348
610-388-6771

These gardens are renowned as
perhaps America's—or even the
world's—premier horticultural
display, with 11,000 different
kinds of plants.

MARYLAND STATE HOUSE

State Circle
Annapolis, MD 21401
410-974-3400

Built from 1772–79, the
Maryland State House is the old-
est state capitol in continuous
legislative use, and it was also the
first peacetime capitol of the
United States. General George
Washington resigned his com-
mission here in 1783. Less than a
month later, the Treaty of Paris
was ratified here, officially ending
the Revolutionary War. The State
House is open to visitors.

NATIONAL TROPICAL BOTANICAL GARDEN

P.O. Box 340
Lawai, Kauai, HI 96756
808-332-7324
808-742-2623 (Tour
Reservations)

Kauai is known as "The Garden
Isle" for all its beautiful flora, and
this is the garden to end all gardens. It's like visiting the Garden
of Eden. The cliffs of the Lawai
Valley were once a retreat for
Hawaii's Queen Emma, and then
in the 1930s, Robert and John
Gregg Allerton transformed the
area into a masterwork of land-
scape that is now the National
Tropical Botanical Garden.

NIZHONI MOSES, LTD

326 San Felipe NW
Old Town
Albuquerque, NM 87104
505-842-1808

Tom Moses helped us understand
his fine selection of Pueblo pot-
tery, Navajo weavings, and much
more when we visited his shop in
the charming Old Town district
of Albuquerque, not far from
Apache Canyon Ranch in
Canoncito, New Mexico.

PHOENIX CENTRE

Route 175
Blue Hill Falls, ME 04615
207-374-2113

Daily kayak tours, fantasy island escapes, multi-day tours, canoe rentals.

PRIVATE PLEASURE

7074 Bembe Beach Road
Annapolis, MD 21403
410-268-9330

This classic, sixty-foot Trumpy motor yacht was built in 1947, and today its new owners serve up an elegant and romantic blend of boat and breakfast—right on the waters of Annapolis! Cruise, dine, and stay overnight in the stateroom aboard a boat not unlike the famed yacht *Sequoia*— also built by John Trumpy and Sons—that served U.S. presidents and their guests.

RENT-A-LOCAL TOURS OF MAUI

Arturo Wesley
333 Dairy Road, Suite 104B
Kahului, Maui, HI 96732
808-877-4042

Custom-designed tours of the island with local guides.

SCHOONER WOODWIND

P.O. Box 3254
Annapolis, MD 21403
410-263-7837

You can sleep overnight on this recently launched 74-foot schooner, which has become the pride of Annapolis—sailing capital of America. Custom-built for the Chesapeake Bay, *Woodwind* offers guests a two-hour sunset sail prior to a romantic evening on board. Bunk down for the night and nod off to the sound of water lapping against the hull. Gourmet continental breakfast the next morning. Daytime sailing tours and charters also available.

TONY NORRIS

Adventures in Story & Song
9475 Doney Park Lane
Flagstaff, AZ 86004
520-526-6684

A cowboy poet, storyteller and singer extraordinaire who appeared on the show.

U.S. NAVAL ACADEMY

Annapolis, MD 21401
410-263-6933

Visitors can tour the U.S. Naval Academy grounds and buildings to enjoy and understand the traditions that date to the academy's beginnings here in 1845.

WHIDBEY WATERWORKS

Frank Pustka
2126 West Madrona Way
Coupeville, WA 98239
360-678-3415

Frank Pustka provides pontoon boats and zodiacs for rent right on Penn Cove at the Captain Whidbey Inn's dock in Coupeville, Washington—a delightful way to enjoy the waters when you're visiting the inn on Whidbey Island near Seattle.

WILLIAM PACA HOUSE

186 Prince George Street
Annapolis, MD 21401
410-263-5553

The restored home and gardens of William Paca—signer of the Declaration of Independence—stand today as one of the most elegant landmarks in historic Annapolis.

WINTERTHUR

Winterthur, DE 19735
302-888-4600

Perhaps the most famous DuPont family estate, Winterthur houses an unrivaled collection of early American decorative arts (1640–1860) displayed in period settings and also boasts a matchless twentieth-century naturalistic garden.

Dining and Lodging

CAPTAIN ISAAC MERRILL INN & CAFE

One Union Street
Blue Hill, ME 04614
207-374-2555

A small B&B right in the heart of the charming coastal Maine village of Blue Hill, serving three meals plus afternoon tea for guests and the general public.

GALAXY DINER

931 West Highway 66
Flagstaff, AZ 86001
520-774-2466

When you're touring the historic highway of America, Route 66, in Flagstaff, as we did during our visit to the Inn at 410, this is the place to get your kicks as well as a cheeseburger, fries, and chocolate shake!

HONU KAI VILLAS

1871 Pe'e Road
Poipu Beach
Kauai, Hawaii 96756
808-742-9155

A great place for an extended stay at Poipu Beach on the south shore of Kauai, especially when Gloria's Spouting Horn B&B is full.

KA'ANAPALI BEACH HOTEL

Lahaina, Maui, HI 96761
808-661-0011

A large hotel with many hands-on traditional Hawaiian cultural activities such as lei-making, hulas dance lessons, and ti-leaf skirt-making.

THE MILLION DOLLAR COWBOY BAR

P.O. Box 621
25 North Cache
Jackson Hole, WY 83001
307-733-2207

A landmark in this town where all good cowgirls and cowboys walk up to a barstool/saddle to quench their thirst, tell tales, and dance.

OLD LAHAINA CAFÉ AND LUAU

505 Front Street
Lahaina, Maui, HI 96761
808-667-1998

Luaus have become rather touristy over the years, but this is one of the closest ever to the real celebration of good food and telling tales through the romantic and poetic dance of the hula.

Fashions

BAGGIT

Pat and Bette Moore
35 West Broadway
Jackson Hole, WY 83001
307-733-1234

An outstanding shop for western women's fashions, some of which we showed off during the show at the Davy Jackson Inn.

THE GECKO STORE

703 Front Street
Lahaina, Maui, HI 96761
808-661-1078

The gecko is a tiny lizard that hangs around homes in Hawaii, bringing good luck to those who reside there. The gecko gets rid of unwanted little prey, so they named a shop after the little critter and sell his image on T-shirts, shorts, caps, and you name it. A delightful grass-hut-looking store that sports a floor of real Hawaiian sand.

HILO HATTIE

Lahaina Center
Lahaina, HI 96761
800-272-5282

The world's largest manufacturer of Hawaiian fashions supplied the wardrobe for the Plantation Inn show in Lahaina on the island of Maui.

SOPHISTICATED YOU

Therese Jasper
Anchor Cove Shopping Center
3416 Rice Street
Lihue, Kauai, HI 96766
808-245-3800

A small women's boutique that supplied the wardrobe for the show at Gloria's Spouting Horn B & B on Kauai.

TELLURIDE TRAPPINGS & TOGGERY

109 E. Colorado Street
Telluride, CO 81435
970-728-3338

Fashionable and functional clothing worn during the episode of the show featuring the San Sophia Inn.

UNC'S BOOT SHOP

Fred (Unc) Ballard
P.O. Box 7944
Jackson, WY 83002
307-733-5477

Custom-made western boots plus boot and shoe repair.

WASHINGTON SQUARE

Kathy Enfoe
2605 Washington Street
Julian, CA 92036
619-765-0861

Unique clothing, jewelry, hats, accessories, dressmaking, and alterations right in the little village of Julian can be found at this shop, which supplied the clothing for the show at Orchard Hill Country Inn.

For the Home and Garden

THE FARMER'S WIFE COMPANY

Julie Schwecke and Lynn
    Bernthal
P.O. Box 3332
Missoula, MT 59806-3332
406-549-1236

Makers of natural, unique soaps
used at Bear Creek Lodge and
sold by mail order. Many of the
soaps are made with ingredients
from the kitchen such as cocoa
for chocolate soap.

LEHUA MAMO FLOWER FARM
AND IRMALEE POMROY FLOWERS

4561 Hokualele Road
P.O. Box 600
Anahola, Kauai, HI 96703-0600
808-822-3231

Lei-making is an art, and few
make them as lovely as Irmalee.
She has won many awards for
her designs.

MRS. McGREGOR'S GARDEN

Sami Mitchell
1017 East Side Highway
Corvallis, MT 59828
406-961-3777

A floral arranger and supplier
extraordinaire who adds her gra-
cious touch to the decor at Bear
Creek Lodge.

NEW HAMPSHIRE HARVEST BARN

100 Black Hill Road
Plainfield, NH 03781
603-644-2783

Supplier of beautiful gift baskets
filled with all manner of goodies
from New Hampshire.

REDBIRD

Box 137
Cochiti, NM 87072
505-465-0911

Maker of wonderful native
American drums—as shown on
the Apache Canyon Ranch
episode.

This book is based on the television series *Country Inn Cooking with Gail Greco,* which is a co-production of Maryland Public Television and Gail Greco.

Trish Crowe is an illustrator and graphic designer who has worked for National Geographic Educational Publications, Revlon, The Discovery Channel, and IBM. She lives in London, England.

Special Thanks To:

No-Stick Systems®

REGAL®

The *Country Inn Cooking with Gail Greco* series on national public television is made possible
by underwriting from DuPont, Jones Dairy Farm, and Regal Ware.
All three have been generous in their support of public television and
the bed-and-breakfast industry.

INNDEX

A

Almond Bread Birds, 140
Almond Cookie Baskets for Peaches and Raspberry Sorbet, 126–127
Anise-Scented Blueberry-and-Peach-Compote, 4
Appetizers
 Artichoke Dip, 132
 Celeriac Chips, 138
 Crawfish in Spicy Creole Sauce, 72
 Oriental Peanut Dip, 132
 Red Pepper Polenta Tostada, 68–69
 Sweet-and-Spicy Shrimp Kebobs Al Fresco, 67
 Tortilla Pinwheels, 69
 Wild Mushroom and Gruyère Potato Latkes, 73
Apple-and-Cheese Toast, 6
Apple-Thyme Chicken, 92
Applewood-Smoked and Rosemary Cornish Hens, 98–99
Apricot-Almond Couscous, 21
Artichoke Dip, 132

B

Bagels, 6–7
Baked Cranberry Oatmeal, 20
Baked Trout Phyllo Bundles with Watercress Sauce, 74–75
Barbecued Marinated Trout with Onion-Caper Relish, 82–83
Beef, Easy Company's-Coming Beef in Puff Pastry, 102–103
Beverages
 Spirited Chocolate Drink, 62
 Tea Latte, 61
Black Bean Salsa, 141
Blueberry Cheese and Lemon-Stuffed Waffles, 37
Breads
 Almond Bread Birds, 140
 Apple-and-Cheese Toast, 6
 bagels, Glacier Bay-Gels, 6–7
 Breakfast Cookies, 9
 Cornbread, 135
 Herbed Focaccia Bread, 134
 Homemade Crusty French Bread, 136–137
 Homemade Pita Bread, 26
 Rose Petal Muffins, 40
 Sausage Applesauce Toast, 5
 Sweet Potato Biscuits with Orange Butter, 8–9
 Tomato-and-Herb Toast, 8
Breakfast Calzone, 13
Breakfast Cookies, 9
Breakfasts
 See also Breads; Fruit
 Baked Cranberry Oatmeal, 20
 Blueberry Cheese and Lemon-Stuffed Waffles, 37
 Breakfast Calzone, 13
 Breakfast Cookies, 9

 Charleston Shrimp 'n' Grits, 22–23
 Cheese-and-Vegetable-Filled Egg Blossom Crêpes, 34
 Coffee-Glazed Cake Cubes with Macadamia Nut Crusts, 45
 Egg-and-Potato Vegetable Tarts with Feta Cheese, 28–29
 Good Morning Pizza, 14–15
 Granola-Peach Breakfast Pie with Yogurt Sauce, 18–19
 Ham-and-Cheese Egg Roll with Parsley Sauce, 30–31
 Herbed Shiitake Eggs in Homemade Pita Bread, 26–27
 Island Eggs Benedict with Mango Salsa, 32–33
 Morning Cheese Pie with Creamed Crabmeat, 17
 Old-Fashioned Fresh Fruit Coffee Cake with Streusel Topping,
  44–45
 Oven Eggs Florentine, 25
 Pancake Pizza with Macadamia Nut Crust and Banana Sour Cream
  Topping, 16
 Papaya Bread Pudding, 12
 Peaches-and-Cream-Stuffed Waffles with Praline Sauce, 36
 Raspberries-and-Cream French Toast with Spiced Peach Sauce,
  38–39
 Sausage, Apple, and Cheese Curried-Cornbread Pudding with
  Pumpkin Sauce, 10–11
 Sausage-and-Cheese-Stuffed Herb Waffles, 35
 Sun-Dried Tomato-and-Bacon Popover Pancake, 24–25
Broccoli Noodle Salad, 53
Broiled Chesapeake Oysters with Roasted Pepper Salsa, 76
Buttermilk Pecan Pie, 115

C

Cakes
 Coffee-Glazed Cake Cubes with Macadamia Nut Crusts, 45
 Oatmeal Tea Cake with Coconut-Pecan Frosting, 63
 Old-Fashioned Fresh Fruit Coffee Cake with Streusel Topping,
  44–45
 Sweet Prune Cakes with Buttermilk Vanilla Sauce, 64
Celeriac Chips, 138
Charleston Shrimp 'n' Grits, 22–23
Cheese-and-Vegetable Filled Egg Blossom Crepês, 34
Chesapeake Crab Cakes, 83
Chicken
 Apple-Thyme Chicken, 92
 Creamed Chicken in Cornbread Cups, 58–59
 Crescent Moon and Star Meat Pasties, 56–57
 Honey-Chili Oriental Fried Chicken, 91
 Peach Chutney with Tarragon Chicken, 94–95
 Saffron-and-Honey-Glazed Medieval Baked Chicken, 93
Chipotle Pork Tenderloin with Apple Tomatillo Sauce, 100–101
Citrus and Roasted Red Pepper Salad with Balsamic Vinaigrette, 47
Coffee-Glazed Cake Cubes with Macadamia Nut Crusts, 45
Cookies
 Almond Cookie Baskets for Peaches and Raspberry Sorbet, 126–127
 Breakfast Cookies, 9

A Cowboy's Chocolate Chip Cookies, 65
Cornbread, 135
Country inns
about, ix–x
directory (page numbers in italics below), 147–157
recipes from
Apache Canyon Ranch, 69, 108, 129, 147
The Ashley Inn, 8–9, 22–23, 26, 35, 37, 141, 147
Bear Creek Lodge, 96–97, 100–101, 132, 134, 137, 147
Blue Hill Inn, 70–71, 85, 86–87, 148
The Captain Freeman Inn, 47, 77, 117, 138–139, 148
The Captain Whidbey Inn, 89, 114, 123, 133, 148
The Cedars Plantation, 49, 58–59, 115, 144, 149
Cousins B&B, 80–81, 90, 91, 111, 143, 149
The Davy Jackson Inn, 63, 64, 104–105, 110–111, 149
Glacier Bay Country Inn, 6–7, 67, 84, 133, 150
Gloria's Spouting Horn B&B Inn, 12, 16, 32–33, 150
The Inn at 410, 10–11, 20, 21, 24–25, 65, 135, 150
The Inn at Maplewood Farm, 1, 3, 4, 26–27, 42–43, 55, 61, 62, 151
The Inn at Montchanin Village, 76, 106, 126–127, 151
Inn at Olde New Berlin, 18–19, 54–55, 78, 102–103, 152
Inn at Le Rosier, 72, 88, 124–125, 152
Inn at Vaucluse Spring, 74–75, 98–99, 120–121, 152
The Notchland Inn, 73, 95, 118–119
Orchard Hill Country Inn, 52, 92, 109, 131, 153
The Plantation Inn/Gerard's Restaurant, 75, 107, 116, 153
Ravenwood Castle, 56–57, 93, 140, 154
San Sophia Inn, 48, 50, 51, 68–69, 138, 154
The Southern Hotel, 9, 14–15, 30–31, 45, 155
The Steamboat Inn, 53, 60, 82–83, 112, 113, 122, 128–129, 132, 141, 155
Victorian Treasure B&B, 28–29, 38–39, 44–45, 156
Washington House Inn, 13, 142, 157
The Wildflower Inn, 34, 40, 144, 145, 156
William Page Inn, 8, 17, 25, 157
Couscous and Wild Rice Pancakes, 112
A Cowboy's Chocolate Chip Cookies, 65
Crabmeat Ravioli with Fresh Tomato Burgundy Sauce, 78
Crackers, Old-Time Soup Crackers, 131
Cranberry Relish, 141
Crawfish in Spicy Creole Sauce, 72
Creamed Chicken in Cornbread Cups, 58–59
Creamy Watermelon-Raspberry Soup, 3
Crescent Moon and Star Meat Pasties, 56–57

D
Desserts
Almond Cookie Baskets for Peaches and Raspberry Sorbet, 126–127
Buttermilk Pecan Pie, 115
A Cowboy's Chocolate Chip Cookies, 65
Hazelnut Orange Shortcake with Blueberry Sauce, 122
Miniature Apple Dumplings, 143
Miss Scarlett's Sorbet, 144
Mocha Chocolate Filbert Pâté with White Chocolate Sauce, 128–129
Oat-Crusted Galette with Cranberry-Apricot Filling, 42–43
Oliebollen, 123
Pecan Beignets with Praline Sauce, 124–125
Raspberry Coulis Cloud, 120–121
Strawberry Swirl Cinnamon-Biscuit Pie, 118–119
Sweet Marsala-Poached Pears with Amaretti Crunch, 117
Sweet Potato Pie, 119
Tortilla Flower Saucers, 129
Tropical Fruit-Filled Pineapple with Meringue Topping, 116
Dill-Dijon Salad Dressing, 133

E
Easy Company's-Coming Beef in Puff Pastry, 102–103
Egg-and-Potato Vegetable Tarts with Feta Cheese, 28–29
Eggs
Cheese-and-Vegetable Filled Egg Blossom Crêpes, 34
Egg-and-Potato Vegetable Tarts with Feta Cheese, 28–29
Ham-and-Cheese Egg Roll with Parsley Sauce, 30–31
Herbed Shiitake Eggs in Homemade Pita Bread, 26–27
Island Eggs Benedict with Mango Salsa, 32–33
Oven Eggs Florentine, 25
Sun-Dried Tomato-and-Bacon Popover Pancake, 24–25

F
Fiddlehead and Lobster Soufflé, 70–71
Fig and Mango Pork Quesadillas, 54
Filet of Elk with Red Currant Sauce, 104–105
Fire-Roasted Salmon with Molasses–Apple Cider Glaze, 89
Flower-Scented Sugar, 144
French Toast, Raspberries-and-Cream French Toast with Spiced Peach Sauce, 38–39
Fruit
Anise-Scented Blueberry-and-Peach Compote, 4
Apricot-Almond Couscous, 21
Creamy Watermelon-Raspberry Soup, 3
Hazelnut Orange Shortcake with Blueberry Sauce, 122
Oat-Crusted Galette with Cranberry-Apricot Filling, 42–43
Port Wine with Fruit Compote, 1
Raspberry Coulis Cloud, 120–121
Spiced Peach Soup, 2
Strawberry-Cantaloupe Side-by-Side Soup, 3
Sweet Marsala-Poached Pears with Amaretti Crunch, 117
Tortilla Flower Saucers, 129

G
Ginger-and-Green Onion Bagels, 7
Glacier Bay-Gels, 6–7

Good Morning Pizza, 14–15
Granola-Peach Breakfast Pie with Yogurt Sauce, 18–19
Grits, Charleston Shrimp 'n' Grits, 22–23

H
Ham-and-Cheese Egg Roll with Parsley Sauce, 30–31
Hazelnut Orange Shortcake with Blueberry Sauce, 122
Herbed Focaccia Bread, 134
Herbed Shiitake Eggs in Homemade Pita Bread, 26–27
Homemade Crusty French Bread, 136–137
Homemade Linguine with Clam Sauce, 79
Homemade Orecchiette Pasta with Broccoli, 77
Homemade Pasta, 138–139
Honey-Chili Oriental Fried Chicken, 91

I
Island Eggs Benedict with Mango Salsa, 32–33
Italian Eggplant Salsa, 142

J
Jalapeño-and-Cheese Bagels, 7
Jams and jellies, Rose Flower Jelly, 145

L
Lamb
Lamb with Roasted-Garlic Beet Risotto, 106
Native-American Lamb Posole, 108
Ragout of Lamb with Garden Vegetables, 107

M
Maple-Glazed Leek, Brie, and Ham Sandwiches, 55
Meats. See Beef; Chicken; Lamb; Pork; Seafood; Turkey; Wild game
Miniature Apple Dumplings, 143
Miss Scarlett's Sorbet, 144
Mocha Chocolate Filbert Pâté with White Chocolate Sauce, 128–129
Molasses-Apple Cider Glaze, 133
Monkfish Medallions with Spinach, Leeks, and Curry, 86–87
Morning Cheese Pie with Creamed Crabmeat, 17

N
Native American Lamb Posole, 108
North Carolina Seafood Gumbo, 80–81

O
Oat-Crusted Galette with Cranberry-Apricot Filling, 42–43
Oatmeal Tea Cake with Coconut-Pecan Frosting, 63
Old-Fashioned Fresh Fruit Coffee Cake with Streusel Topping, 44–45
Old-Time Soup Crackers, 131
Oliebollen, 123
Oriental Peanut Dip, 132
Oven Eggs Florentine, 25

P
Pancake Pizza with Macadamia Nut Crust and Banana Sour Cream
   Topping, 16
Papaya Bread Pudding, 12
Pasta
Crabmeat Ravioli with Fresh Tomato Burgundy Sauce, 78
Homemade Linguine with Clam Sauce, 79
Homemade Orecchiette Pasta with Broccoli, 77
Homemade Pasta, 138–139
Spicy Three-Cheese Baked Macaroni, 111
Toasted Noodle and Rice Pilaf, 109
Peach Chutney with Tarragon Chicken, 94–95
Peaches-and-Cream-Stuffed Waffles with Praline Sauce, 35
Pecan Beignets with Praline Sauce, 124–125
Pecan and Romaine Salad with Sweet-and-Sour Dressing, 49
Pies
Buttermilk Pecan Pie, 115
Strawberry Swirl Cinnamon-Biscuit Pie, 118–119
Sweet Potato Pie, 119
meat, Crescent Moon and Star Meat Pasties, 56–57
Pork
Chipotle Pork Tenderloin with Apple Tomatillo Sauce, 100–101
Ham-and-Cheese Egg Roll with Parsley Sauce, 30–31
Sausage, Apple, and Cheese Curried-Cornbread Pudding with
   Pumpkin Sauce, 10–11
Sausage Applesauce Toast, 5
Sausage-and-Cheese-Stuffed Herb Waffles, 35
Port Wine with Fruit Compote, 1
Potatoes
Roasted-Garlic Mashed Potatoes with Basil and Sun-Dried Tomatoes,
   113
Wild Mushroom and Gruyère Potato Latkes, 73
Wild Wyoming Potato and Vegetable Compote, 110–111
Wolffish in Potato Crust with Chervil Sauce, 85
Puddings
Papaya Bread Pudding, 12
Sausage, Apple, and Cheese Curried-Cornbread Pudding with
   Pumpkin Sauce, 10–11

R
Ragout of Lamb with Garden Vegetables, 107
Raspberries-and-Cream French Toast with Spiced Peach Sauce, 38–39
Raspberry Coulis Cloud, 120–121
Red Bean Succotash, 114
Red Pepper Polenta Tostada, 68–69
Rice
Couscous and Wild Rice Pancakes, 112
Toasted Noodle and Rice Pilaf, 109
Roasted Garlic, 137
Roasted-Garlic Mashed Potatoes with Basil and Sun-Dried Tomatoes,
   113

Roasted Grouper with Smoked Tomato Butter Sauce, 88
Roasted Red Pepper and Fennel Salad, 48
Roasted Vegetable and Corn Milk Chili, 96–97
Rose Flower Jelly, 145
Rose Petal Muffins, 40

S
Saffron-and-Honey-Glazed Medieval Baked Chicken, 93
Salads
    Broccoli Noodle Salad, 53
    Citrus and Roasted Red Pepper Salad with Balsamic Vinaigrette, 47
    Pecan and Romaine Salad with Sweet-and-Sour Dressing, 49
    Roasted Red Pepper and Fennel Salad, 48
    Shrimp Papaya Salad in Avocado with Mango-Macadamia Dressing, 52
    Warm Spinach Salad with Nectarine Vinaigrette, 50
    Wilted Salad with Walnuts, Pear, Stilton, and Orange Vinaigrette, 51
Sandwiches
    Crescent Moon and Star Meat Pasties, 56–57
    Fig and Mango Pork Quesadillas, 54–55
    Maple-Glazed Leek, Brie, and Ham Sandwiches, 55
    Turkey Croissant Sandwiches with Cranberry Relish, 60
Sauces and dressings
    Apple Tomatillo Sauce, 100
    Basting Sauce, 67
    Black Bean Salsa, 141
    Buttermilk Vanilla Sauce, 64
    Chervil Sauce, 85
    Clam Sauce, 79
    Cranberry Relish, 141
    Dill-Dijon Salad Dressing, 133
    Fig Gravy, 90
    Fresh Tomato Burgundy Sauce, 78
    Italian Eggplant Salsa, 142
    Mango Salsa, 32
    Mango-Macadamia Dressing, 52
    Molasses–Apple Cider Glaze, 133
    Nectarine Vinaigrette, 50
    Olive-Chili Relish, 84
    Onion-Caper Relish, 82–83
    Orange Butter, 8
    Orange Vinaigrette, 51
    Red Currant Sauce, 104–105
    Roasted Pepper Salsa, 76
    Smoked Tomato Butter Sauce, 88
    Sweet-and-Sour Dressing, 49
    Watercress Sauce, 74
    White Chocolate Sauce, 128
Sausage, Apple, and Cheese Curried-Cornbread Pudding with Pumpkin Sauce, 10–11
Sausage Applesauce Toast, 5

Sausage-and-Cheese-Stuffed Herb Waffles, 35
Sautéed Halibut with Olive-Chili Relish, 84
Seafood
    Baked Trout Phyllo Bundles with Watercress Sauce, 74–75
    Barbecued Marinated Trout with Onion-Caper Relish, 82–83
    Broiled Chesapeake Oysters with Roasted Pepper Salsa, 76
    Charleston Shrimp 'n' Grits, 22–23
    Chesapeake Crabcakes, 83
    Crabmeat Ravioli with Fresh Tomato Burgundy Sauce, 78
    Crawfish in Spicy Creole Sauce, 72
    Fiddlehead and Lobster Soufflè, 70–71
    Fire-Roasted Salmon with Molasses–Apple Cider Glaze, 89
    Homemade Linguine with Clam Sauce, 79
    Monkfish Medallions with Spinach, Leeks and Curry, 86–87
    Morning Cheese Pie with Creamed Crabmeat, 17
    North Carolina Seafood Gumbo, 80–81
    Roasted Grouper with Smoked Tomato Butter Sauce, 88
    Sautéed Halibut with Olive-Chili Relish, 84
    Seared Tuna and Snapper with Wild Fennel, 75
    Shark with Fig Gravy, 90
    Shrimp Papaya Salad in Avocado with Mango-Macadamia Dressing, 52
    Sweet-and-Spicy Shrimp Kebobs al Fresco, 67
    Wolf-fish in Potato Crust with Chervil Sauce, 85
Seared Tuna and Snapper with Wild Fennel, 75
Shark with Fig Gravy, 90
Shrimp Papaya Salad in Avocado with Mango-Macadamia Dressing, 52
Soups and stews
    crackers for, Old-Time Soup Crackers, 131
    Creamy Watermelon-Raspberry Soup, 3
    North Carolina Seafood Gumbo, 80–81
    Roasted Vegetable and Corn Milk Chili, 96–97
    Southwest Country-Style Rabbit Stew, 95
    Spiced Peach Soup, 2
    Strawberry-Cantaloupe Side-by-Side Soup, 3
Southwest Country-Style Rabbit Stew, 95
Spiced Peach Soup, 2
Spicy Three-Cheese Baked Macaroni, 111
Spirited Chocolate Drink, 62
Strawberry Swirl Cinnamon-Biscuit Pie, 118–119
Strawberry-Cantaloupe Side-by-Side Soup, 3
Sugar, Flower-Scented, 144
Sun-Dried Tomato-and-Basil Bagels, 7
Sun-Dried Tomato-and-Bacon Popover Pancake, 24–25
Sweet Marsala–Poached Pears with Amaretti Crunch, 117
Sweet Potato Biscuits with Orange Butter, 8–9
Sweet Potato Pie, 119
Sweet Prune Cakes with Buttermilk Vanilla Sauce, 64
Sweet-and-Spicy Shrimp Kebobs al Fresco, 67
T
Tea Latte, 61

Toasted Noodle and Rice Pilaf, 109
Toasts, breakfast, about, 5
Tortilla Flower Saucers, 129
Tortilla Pinwheels, 69
Tropical Fruit-Filled Pineapple with Meringue Topping, 116
Turkey Croissant Sandwiches with Cranberry Relish, 60

V
Vegetables
See also Potatoes; Salads
Cheese-and-Vegetable-Filled Egg Blossom Crêpes, 34
Ragout of Lamb with Vegetables, 107
Red Bean Succotash, 114
Roasted Vegetable and Corn Milk Chili, 96–97
Wild Wyoming Potato and Vegetable Compote, 110–111

W
Waffles
Blueberry Cheese-and-Lemon-Stuffed Waffles, 37
Peaches-and-Cream-Stuffed Waffles with Praline Sauce, 35
Sausage-and-Cheese-Stuffed Herb Waffles, 36
Warm Spinach Salad with Nectarine Vinaigrette, 50
Wild game
Applewood-Smoked and Rosemary Cornish Hens, 98–99
Filet of Elk with Red Currant Sauce, 104–105
Southwest Country-Style Rabbit Stew, 95
Wild Mushroom and Gruyére Potato Latkes, 73
Wild Wyoming Potato and Vegetable Compote, 110–111
Wilted Salad with Walnuts, Pear, Stilton, and Orange Vinaigrette, 51
Wolf-fish in Potato Crust with Chervil Sauce, 85